The New Game Plan:

Using Sports to Raise Happy, Healthy, and Successful Kids

Stephen R. Raghoobarsingh, M.A.

Trafford
PUBLISHING

This book is dedicated to my amazing group of family and friends.

Mom, thank you for being such a guiding light in my life. Through your brilliant warmth and direction I learned early on that my dreams were simply realities in waiting. You taught me to always trust my instincts and that love was unconditional, no exceptions. Thanks for shaping me to become the person that I am today.

Dad, thank you for teaching me to appreciate life in the moment. You're an amazing example of how to be both hard working and easygoing. You've always known how to put a smile on a person's face and can make any stranger feel right at home. Thanks for helping me create the path that I am on today.

Roger, you are the most amazing brother a guy could ever hope for. You're my best friend, sports buddy, and the one I've looked up to my whole life. All my favourite childhood memories have you in it and I wouldn't change them for the world. Thanks for all of your support and for always having my back.

I also want to thank my incredible friends and relatives. You've all been such a terrific source of love and support. The times we have shared together have been so inspiring and will continue to have a profound impact on me.

Thank you and God bless you all!

ACKNOWLEDGEMENTS

Dad, Mom, Roger

The Raghoobarsingh Family

The Seebaran Family

The Gunaratna Family

The Pregler Family

My Trinidad Family

Phil Knapp

Aeron McKie

Gary Seebaran

Ramin Shadmehr

Brad MacLean

Sarina Perneel

Sean Ramjagsingh

Ron Ganase

Ravi Ramnarine

Dave Larocque

Kelly Nault

Josh Bath

Rainy, Joe, Katy, and Gavin

Tyler Newbery

Corrine Lee

Suzanne Kyra

Frank Quarto

Christie Vairo

Doug Okabe

Johnny Gazzola

Karla Sims

Sandy Jagday

Bal Sandhu

Ian, Seb, James

Matt Greeley

Jag Minhas

Sicily

Khalib and Jaiden

Josh, Jacob, Jada

Nyesha, Mckia, Immanuel

Kaila, Blakey, Brandon, Emily

Tianna

Vanessa, Anjali, Justin

Brendon and Briana

TABLE OF CONTENTS

INTRODUCTION

The Athlete's Paradox

" You've got to be kidding!" I muttered to myself in disbelief. If I didn't know any better, I'd say these sports pages were sounding more and more like a bad Hollywood script. Even more disappointing for me was the fact that I waited two whole weeks to rifle through this stack of papers. You see, as a sports counsellor, I often travel out-of-town to conduct workshops and work with clients, including young children, elite athletes, parents, coaches, and so on. But one of the things I really look forward to upon my return is getting caught up on all of the latest on-field action. Unfortunately, on this day, it was the off-field action that was taking centre stage.

After realizing the magnitude of the headlines before me, I found myself just sitting at the patio table a bit stunned and perplexed. Fortunately, my little nephew Blake, who was playing soccer outside with a few of his friends, broke the silence by shouting, "Watch me, Uncle!" I quickly got up to cheer on "Blakey" and his friends and, as I watched them playing joyfully, it dawned on me. If the cream of the crop in professional sports were committing rapes, murders, and abusing drugs, how could I ever live with myself if I were to guide any youngster to even the slightest threat of this "unhealthy" lifestyle? It was at that moment that I decided to devote my entire career to help parents, coaches, and teachers learn about using sports to positively affect their children's futures.

So, where to begin? Well, for starters, we need to understand that the "athlete's paradox" is perhaps the biggest problem in the sporting world today. Even if your children are doing "fine" in sports, or are not playing at a high level, the athlete's paradox will still affect them because of how embedded it is in the sporting world and that includes our parenting and coaching styles.

In a nutshell, the athlete's paradox is the contradiction that children face when they realize that their same approach accepted "on" the field is not accepted "off" the field. In other words, children are being taught to behave a certain way on the field, the court, and the rink and then taught that that same behaviour is inappropriate at school, on the playground, and at home. Confusing don't you think? Professional athletes aren't the only ones that receive these mixed messages. Remember they were once children, too. In schools, there are countless children everywhere who get away with cheating on tests or are allowed to skip out on exams because they are "athletes." What types of messages are we sending them? The "not so funny" thing is that the people who allow this to happen are the same people who end up shunning our kids years later when they are discovered to be illiterate or are found begging for careers. Something needs to be done now, so that we aren't setting up the next generation for failure.

But the question still remains, "Why do we let this happen"? Well, the athlete's paradox has a lot to do with us being blinded by the prospect of status, fame, fortune, or prestige when we spot children who have a talent for their sport. The lure of athletic achievements, regardless of the level of play, carries so much weight in today's society that it tends to warp our perspective in some very unfortunate ways. In many instances, this warped perspective forces us to turn a blind eye to the abuse our children endure, in subtle or not so subtle ways, and causes us to rationalize their mistreatment as "just a part of their training." It doesn't end here. Our children are often forced to witness their sporting heroes using drugs to cheat, or their "role-model" parents assaulting, and in some cases killing, other parents at sporting events. We need to grasp that this "winning-at-all-costs" mentality will not take our children to the promised land of "gold medals" or "number one" status. In fact, I can attest that no benefit ever comes from the winning-at-all-costs approach, only harm.

Fortunately, this book will not only address the athlete's paradox, but it will guide your children's lifelong sports participation at any level. Whether you're a parent, teacher, counsellor, or an athlete, this book will help you re-evaluate the true nature of sporting activities as well as help you use sports to raise happy, healthy, and successful kids! Along the way, you'll discover a ground-breaking model of sports and innovative ways of structuring athletic activities that will positively impact your child's overall development. You'll even read some enlightening stories of children who were empowered by this new approach to benefit their lives both on and off the field.

Now, you may find that I pay a lot of attention to the more popular sports in North America, but keep in mind that the book's concepts apply to every sport and every recreational activity. You'll also find that each chapter contains some very special features. "Top 7s" are checklists full of helpful hints to be taken and used right away. "Chalk Talks" offer further insight into the concepts being discussed. And "Extra Innings" shed light on the hottest topics today in the sporting world.

Hope you enjoy embarking on this one-of-a-kind literary road trip. Are you ready? Get set...let's go!

CHAPTER 1

The Secret To Working With Kids

Wherever I go, whether it's at a parenting workshop, a coaching seminar, a consultation, or even a youth conference, I am often asked, "What do you think is the secret to working with kids?" My answer? The ability to fully develop *Social Interest*. But what exactly is Social Interest? As I define it, Social Interest is all about *moving together towards a common goal while balancing the needs of the individual with the needs of the group.* This concept basically points to our ability to take great care of ourselves while being a great source of support for others. Each one of us has the capacity to develop Social Interest, and when our children develop it, they put themselves on a path to social, emotional, and mental health. Developing the ability to balance individual needs with group needs is a major part of enhancing one's self-esteem and will impact every major aspect of one's life. Take a few moments to reflect on some of the happiest memories in your life. If you recalled cherished memories of you experiencing things alone, or amazing moments shared amongst family, friends, teammates, and so on, you wouldn't be the only one. These memories which reflect personal growth and a sense of community are what Social Interest is all about.

So what does Social Interest have to do with sports? Well, quite a lot actually. In fact, participation in sports is a great way of developing Social Interest. All you have to do is look at the amount of teamwork that goes into your son's soccer playoff drive, or your daughter's softball championship, to know that it exists. Believe it or not, up until now, nothing has ever been written on the subject. Despite all of the literature on the physical, social, and general psychological aspects of sports, Social Interest and its obvious relationship to sports has never been officially discussed. This lack of academic investigation presented me with a tremendous opportunity. It gave me the chance to combine my passion for sports with my sincere belief in Social Interest. The final product, you ask? Well, how about a brand new theory of sports that will forever change the way we view athletics? The name of this original theory is *The New Game Plan,* and after we take the time to understand its connection to our children's self-esteem, we'll be better equipped to tackle the athlete's paradox. In this book, self-esteem will be defined as *the belief a child has in his or her own ability or value.* As you'll see, it is directly influenced by sport and can be nurtured through healthy participation in a variety of athletic activities.

As you go through *The New Game Plan* theory, I strongly recommend that you carefully go over its concepts, since they truly underlie every section and chapter in this book. For those of you who do not have children in sports, bear in mind that the theory's principles are also applicable to extra-curricular activities. We'll take a look at the theory's application to drama, band, chess, and so forth a little later on in this chapter's "Chalk Talk." However, in the interest of keeping things simple, our focus will be solely on sporting activities.

The Sporty Side Of Social Interest

To help out with this section, I thought it might be fun for you to get inside my head for a few minutes and recall with me some of the questions I had when putting together *The New Game Plan*. If you find this part of the book a little more formal, I apologize ahead of time, but remember that it sets the stage for the pages to follow. So for the next few minutes feel free to pull up a chair, grab a beverage, and read away.

Alright then, if we intend to create a brand new theory of sports that covers every sport we can think of, this is the first question we need to ask:

"What do all sports have in common?"

This question makes complete sense because, in order to compare sports, we need to know the similarities that exist between each of them. Now, I caught myself asking this question out loud to Blakey who wasted no time at all in shouting, "Uniforms, sport drinks, gum…" you get the idea. Although Blakey's suggestions were amusing to hear, his remarks were a nice reminder that I had to ask more direct questions if the theory were to focus on more meaningful aspects of sports. Here is the first of these more direct questions:

"What is the primary objective of any sport?"

How would you answer this? If you said something along the lines of "to win," you'd be on the right track, for sure. Now, here's the second of these more direct questions:

"How do you measure winning?"

The answer to this might be a little more difficult. If you responded with the phrases, "by scoring," "the offensive side of sports," or "the scoring process," each would be correct. That's because they all reflect standards based on time, points, distance, and so on. Whichever phrase you decide to use will be of utmost importance in *The New Game Plan* theory because each one answers the very first question we asked at the beginning of the section: "What do all sports have in common?"

I can hear some people asking, "What about the defensive side of sports?" Well, even though the defensive side is extremely important, it isn't found in every sport, so to compare athletic activities using this side of sports would be unfair. Here's what I mean. Would it make sense to compare the defensive side of hockey to golf, which doesn't have one? The answer is "no."

Now, if you're thinking that this theory should be emphasizing the "fun" aspects of sport, I would agree wholeheartedly. But at this point, in order to establish a general theory, we need to look at things that are purely objective and researchable. "Fun" is subjective and unresearchable. Nevertheless, I promise that taking the time to understand the objective side will allow us to appreciate the subjective side that much more.

Okay then, with the scoring process as our main focus, we are now in a position to examine the value of the scoring object or measuring tool. The scoring object is what every athlete's motivations and efforts are directed towards in the scoring process. It not only refers to a hockey puck, a soccer ball, or a football, but the length of a jump, the time established in a race, and so on. It's impossible to discuss the scoring process without referring to the scoring object.

The scoring process or the offensive side of sports finally gives us the common denominator we've been looking for, and it allows us to begin to apply Social Interest to sports. If you recall, Social Interest is about *moving together towards a common goal*. When we relate this principle to sports, it can be reasoned that the *common goal* is to win, and the *moving together towards* this goal is the scoring process. This leads us to ask one final question:

"During the scoring process, what are the different types of interaction that occur in relation to the scoring object?"

In other words, what are the possible ways of scoring? There are, in fact, three possible ways of scoring that occur between teammates in relation to the scoring object. I often refer to them as levels of interaction or forms of Social Interest, and they include direct interaction, communication, and isolated play.

"Direct Interaction" Leads To So Much Satisfaction!

So what is *direct interaction*? Simply put, it's the actual physical exchange of a scoring object between teammates. It contributes to the *needs of the group* aspect of Social Interest and is the part of the game that has raised us out of our seats on numerous occasions. Evgeni Malkin "passing the puck" up the ice to Sidney Crosby in hockey, or Peyton Manning "throwing the pigskin" down the field to Marvin Harrison in football are considered by many of us, who have watched these amazing athletes, to be the height of direct interaction.

Direct interaction, however, may not be as obvious in other sports. In team rowing, the boat is the object and it is moved through the collective rowing of the rowers who are always in direct contact with it.

Now, we have to be careful not to confuse direct interaction between teammates with the competition that occurs between "opponents." In hockey, when Wade Belak takes the ice against Donald Brashear, these two burly hockey players are there to oppose one another. Their interaction has nothing at all to do with *moving together towards a common goal*. In fact, the two of them may even get into a physical confrontation if they believe it will prevent the other team from winning. That's why competition between players is not the same as direct interaction between teammates. Competition pits you against me, but direct interaction brings the two of us together. Competition is a necessary aspect of sport and life, and using it productively depends a lot on the way in which we use the principles of this theory. So, stay tuned!

Athletes Need To "Communicate" Too

When you play baseball, cricket, or participate in curling, direct interaction isn't allowed during the offensive side of these games, but *communication* is. Communication, which can be either verbal or non-verbal, contributes to the *needs of the group* aspect of Social Interest and I often refer to it as indirect interaction. Remember, only the offensive side of the game is highlighted when we compare sports because the defensive side doesn't exist in every activity. With this in mind, indirect interaction in baseball may look like Derek Jeter responding to a hand sign or running from 1st to 2nd base because of a hit at the plate by Bernie Williams, his teammate. Now, if Derek Jeter came into direct contact with the baseball (the scoring object) immediately after it was hit by Bernie Williams during the offensive side of an inning, he would be penalized or called "out" by the umpire.

In curling, a sweeper can assist the stone (the scoring object) to the tee (the scoring area) after it has been delivered by a teammate. However, just as in baseball, if the sweeper makes direct contact with the stone while sweeping, the team will be penalized.

When we acknowledge sweeping as a form of indirect interaction, we aren't suggesting that it requires less skill or expertise than direct interaction. It's a simple comment on the relationship between the stone and members of the same curling team. We also need to note that indirect interaction may reflect the tallying up of scores from separate athletes. If one golfer's round of 68 is added to another golfer's round of 70 on the same golf team, their "score-combination" of 138 represents indirect interaction since each round was played independent of each other before being added.

<u>Last, But Certainly Not Least..."Isolated Play"</u>

Some of the greatest moments in sports history are *isolated plays*. Isolated play represents an individual performance that occurs without direct interaction and communication and contributes to the *needs of the individual* aspect of Social Interest. Tiger Woods making that big "chip shot" in a playoff hole to win the Masters Golf Tournament, and Joe Carter smashing a home run to win the World Series for the Toronto Blue Jays are just two memorable examples of this very exciting part of the game. For the rest of us, instances of isolated play occur everyday on our playgrounds and in our sports fantasies. I'm sure many of you have dreamt about making that final basket at the sound of the buzzer, or have caught that last-second touchdown in your very own backyard. Whatever the scenario, isolated play has long been a cherished part of sports and receives a great deal of attention from us and from our sports historians.

Re-Designing The Sports Landscape

Applying Social Interest to the field of sports forces us to change our point-of-view. For starters, take the way we traditionally categorize athletics. Instead of just labeling them as "individual" or "team" sports, based solely on the general number of participants, *The New Game Plan* allows us to categorize athletics with a lot more purpose and meaning. In fact, direct interaction, communication, and isolated play give us a chance to re-design the landscape of sports, in a manner of speaking. These three levels of interaction actually expand upon the two traditional basic labels and offer us three new, dynamic categories. The first category is "team sports," and in *The New Game Plan* framework, this category reflects activities that allow direct interaction, communication, and isolated play:

Team Sports

Direct Interaction: **Yes**
Communication: **Yes**
Isolated Play: **Yes**

Examples: basketball, hockey, soccer, football, rugby, volleyball, field hockey, lacrosse

The second category is "pseudo-team sports." It's the newest sports category, and it represents athletic activities that do not allow direct interaction, but do allow communication and isolated play:

Pseudo-Team Sports

Direct Interaction: No
Communication: **Yes**
Isolated Play: **Yes**

Examples: baseball, softball, cricket, curling, doubles tennis, team golf, swimming relays

The third category is "individual sports," and it consists of single participant activities that offer us the opportunity to use isolated play on its own:

Individual Sports

Direct Interaction: No
Communication: No
Isolated Play: **Yes**

Examples: golf, singles tennis, bowling, running, racquetball, figure skating, squash, downhill skiing, snowboarding, gymnastics, javelin

Top 7 Ways Parents Can Apply The New Game Plan

1. Family Activities
- *team*: doing the dishes (one person washes, the other person dries), preparing meals
- *pseudo-team*: cleaning up the house (everyone is responsible for cleaning one area or room), family meetings, grocery shopping
- *individual*: taking out the trash, mowing the lawn

2. Social Activities
- *team*: cubs, scouts, girl guides
- *pseudo-team*: group karaoke, group nature walks
- *individual*: travelling, going to the movies

3. School Activities
- *team*: group projects, tutoring, mentoring
- *pseudo-team*: group presentations, choir
- *individual*: painting, drawing, writing

4. Physical Training
- *team*: weight-training with a partner, stretching with a partner
- *pseudo-team*: group runs, group hikes
- *individual*: yoga, aerobics

5. Extra-Curricular Activities
- *team*: team canoeing, team mountain climbing
- *pseudo-team*: group puzzles, group board games
- *individual*: spelling bees, chess

6. Coaching Activities
- *team*: team drills, team strength-training
- *pseudo-team*: parent meetings, team meetings, fundraisers
- *individual*: personal training, one-to-one meetings

7. Recreation Programs
- *team*: youth dances, outdoor group adventures
- *pseudo-team*: youth committees, youth forums
- *individual*: dance programs, babysitter training programs, cooking programs

To quickly summarize, we know that children experience three forms of Social Interest in a team sport, two forms in a pseudo-team sport, and one in an individual sport. We also know that baseball, cricket, and curling are no longer identified as team sports, and their change in classification to pseudo-team sports isn't to be viewed as a step down. The change simply reflects the way these activities are organized under the microscope of a sports theory that uses objective criteria. The term "pseudo-team" is used because it represents athletic groups that appear as teams, but they aren't teams because they don't allow players to interact directly during the scoring process (which, if you recall, is our focus when we compare sports).

Chalk Talk: *The New Game Plan* And Non-Athletic Activities

If you're a parent of children who do not play sports, *The New Game Plan* theory can still be applied to non-athletic activities. For example, drama/theatre and group arts and crafts fall under the team category because they allow your children to experience all three forms of Social Interest. Choir and band are suited to the pseudo-team category because they expose your children to communication and isolated play. Finally, chess and solo music lessons fit under the individual category because they promote isolated play. Relating non-athletic activities to *The New Game Plan* theory in this way is important in order for your children to still benefit from the theory's concepts and applications without participating in sports.

After rummaging around in my head for a bit, you may be left wondering, "What does all of this stuff mean?" Well, for the first time ever, sport can be organized using clear, objective criteria. In other words, we can use sport as a teaching tool to build our children's self-esteem and enhance their overall development. Have you ever heard of the saying, "sport is a vehicle for life?"

Well, it takes on greater meaning now that our athletes from the grass-roots level to the professional ranks can use sport to purposefully enhance their lives. Chapter 2 lets us in on how this process begins, but not before we end this chapter with our first Extra Inning.

EXTRA INNING:

Why We Don't See That Many Upsets In Baseball!

With our new theory of sports in place, we are now in a position to discuss athletics in a way that we never could before. Take a look at baseball, for example. *The New Game Plan* theory separates it from other team sports because it offers communication and isolated play, but not direct interaction. Believe it or not, this actually explains why we don't see that many upsets on the baseball diamond in comparison to other pro sports in North America. Do you recall the Detroit Pistons defeating the heavily favoured Los Angeles Lakers in the 2004 National Basketball Association (NBA) Finals? Do you remember the Calgary Flames 2004 Stanley Cup run that saw them defeat three regular season division champions before losing in a thrilling 7-game series final? What about upsets in Major League Baseball (MLB)? Well, there's really not much to talk about in this sport when it comes to upsets. And before you reference the *Bad News Bears*, remember that was just a movie!

Sure, there are some pleasant surprises such as the Boston Red Sox winning the World Series after 86 years of futility, but can you really classify a club with an average of 95 wins in each of its last 3 seasons leading up to its title as an upset? The Red Sox victory doesn't even come close to the US Olympic Hockey team defeating the powerful Russian squad at Lake Placid on their way to gold in 1980.

So why the discrepancy between baseball and the other big league sports? Well, as mentioned, baseball isn't a team sport that allows direct interaction. When athletes, playing a team sport, are allowed to work in direct concert with one another, a whole new dynamic is created. On-field plays and coaching strategies become more complex when direct interaction is involved, and they serve as great equalizers for underdog teams going up against mighty powerhouses. Game plans in baseball just don't have the team element found in hockey plays, football schemes, or basketball offences. Success in these team sports is built on team strategy, as much as it is on individual skill, and requires players to interact extremely well in a variety of direct ways.

So how does this explain the lack of upsets? Well, since baseball is based on communication and isolated play, it follows that skill and talent cannot be counteracted in the same way that they are in team sports. That's why the New York Yankees have been the premiere club in the major leagues for the past 10 years or so. This club looks for available talent and then goes out and buys it. In baseball, it's a pretty safe bet that if you have the most talented players on your club, you'll be pretty difficult to beat because there is no direct interaction to offset your skill level or talent base. This isn't the case in the other professional leagues. Just ask the New York Rangers. They've tried to mimic their baseball counterparts by purchasing high-priced talent and have been a perennial payroll leader in the National Hockey League (NHL) for several years before the NHL lockout began. Unfortunately, between 1997 and the time this labour dispute occurred, the Rangers were unable to make the playoffs. Even in the National Football League (NFL), the unheralded Baltimore Ravens, Tampa Bay Buccaneers, and New England Patriots have been the last few Super Bowl Champions. These teams won because of their ability to work well as a group, not just because of their talent. In fact, the New England

Patriots are establishing a dynasty with a roster full of role players who are well-renowned for their dedication to teamwork.

In baseball, the Yankees' closest rivals for the past 10 years have been the Atlanta Braves and Boston Red Sox who (surprise, surprise) have been up there with the Yankees in the payroll department. Purchasing power translates to wins in baseball. But there is some hope, however, for the other teams in the majors. They can combat high-priced talent by first seeking out unproven talent in the minors and then by emphasizing the indirect interaction aspects of the game in hopes of making the playoffs. This philosophy has paid off for the Oakland Athletics and Florida Marlins, who have made it to the post-season in recent years; and in the Marlins' case, it has led to two World Series titles. Unfortunately, once their unproven talent becomes "proven," the lure of big money contracts from the bigger-market clubs becomes way too much for the smaller-market teams to bear. Teams, such as the Athletics and Marlins, end up waving "goodbye" to many of the young stars they took the time to groom and ultimately have to begin looking for unproven talent once again. You wouldn't be out of line in suggesting that many of the MLB franchises are feeder teams for the bigger payroll clubs. This may be true in other pro leagues as well, but, at least, the Flames and the Pistons have a chance to compete with the highly skilled teams in their sports because of direct interaction. (Check out the "Extra Inning" at the end of the next chapter to read about some suggestions that will help professional leagues balance payrolls and level the financial playing field without doing any harm to their sports.)

CHAPTER 2:

Sport As A Life Tool

The reason why sport isn't given the official credit it deserves for its role in one's overall development is simple: there has been no official theory of sports, that is, up until now. With *The New Game Plan* in place, we can begin to understand the many ways in which each sport impacts our children's lives. In fact, we can begin to make some really good guesses about the sports best suited for our children in order to help them build their self-esteem. Many of you may have begun to think about this already, and with what we know up to this point, some of you may suggest that team sports are better to play because they offer all three forms of Social Interest. But nothing could be further from the truth. Allow me to explain this with a little "pizza" talk.

Pizza And Psychology

If we agree that every child is unique, then we have to agree that his or her psychological make-up is unique too. Funny enough, I usually relate this topic to pizza. For those of you who enjoy eating pizza, it's unlikely that we all share the same "tastes" in toppings. I'm sure many of you enjoy veggie toppings on your pizzas, while others, myself included, prefer the love-it or leave-it combination of pepperoni and anchovies. These "tastes" which influence our choice of pizzas are very similar to our "beliefs" which influence our choice of sports. In other words, the sports that our children play say a great deal about their beliefs.

Imagine, for a moment, craving your favourite pizza but being forced to eat one that you couldn't stomach at all. This happens quite regularly in sports too. On many occasions, we place our children in athletic activities that really don't support their positive self-beliefs or "I-am messages." I-am messages refer to the beliefs we carry around in our heads all of the time. You may have heard them referred to as "self-talk," but regardless of the term that is used, they reflect the way we truly feel about ourselves. I-am messages can either be positive or negative, and the chances of them being positive dramatically increase when children approach athletic activities with the intention of having fun, developing skills, and improving themselves.

So, how do you go about finding out what your children's I-am messages are? Well, the trick is to look at their current behaviour and make guesses about where they are at from a mental perspective. For example, when you think about your child, you may ask, "Does my child tend to isolate him or herself from others?" If the answer is "yes," then chances are he or she believes "I am alone." "I am alone" in this case is a negative I-am message since the isolation that comes with this belief stems from being unable to socialize well with others. It's a message that is quite different from the more positive "I am independent" message, which reflects self-care and self-sufficiency rather than avoidance from social settings. If your child possesses the "I am alone" message, he or she would benefit greatly from participation in team sports and pseudo-team sports (see the I-am messages associated with each type of sport later on in this section). But remember, it is still important to nurture the "I am independent" belief through healthy participation in individual sports.

On the flip side, you may ask something along the lines of, "Does my child lack independence or self-reliance?" If the answer to this question is "yes," then your child likely believes "I am incapable," and individual sports may play an important role in his or her development.

The point of all of this is to show that team sports, although important to your child's development, may not necessarily be the most appropriate choice for your child. In fact, participation in different types of sports is the key to establishing a healthy balance in life. Let's re-visit our pizza scenario for a moment. If we were on a pizza-only diet and were only able to order one type of pizza, would we achieve the nutritional balance that our bodies needed? Of course, we wouldn't. The same principle applies to our children's athletic participation. The more types of sports they play, the more well-rounded they will be. To assist you in making decisions around their sports involvement, here's an outline of some of the positive I-am messages associated with each type of sport:

Team Sports
I <u>am</u> social
I <u>am</u> contributing
I <u>am</u> competent
I <u>am</u> interacting well with others

Pseudo-Team Sports
I <u>am</u> part of a group
I <u>am</u> capable
I <u>am</u> communicating well with others

Individual Sports
I <u>am</u> self-reliant
I <u>am</u> independent
I <u>am</u> responsible

To illustrate the importance of strategically planning your child's athletic participation, here are two real-life stories of children who benefited from *The New Game Plan* approach. The names of these two amazing children (and the names of every other child referred to throughout the book, Blakey excluded) have been changed to protect their identities.

<u>Daniel's "Basketball Shoot-Out"</u>

For the great number of children out there, who isolate themselves because of an "I am alone" message, it's important to help them build their self-esteem and achieve life balance with increased participation in team and pseudo-team sports. However, before they begin moving in this direction, they need to start out where they feel most comfortable. Usually, for children seeking to be alone, safety and comfort can be found in individual sports through isolated play.

To illustrate what I mean, let me tell you about my work with Daniel. When I first met Daniel, it was hard not to notice his size. As a 6 year-old, he was quite underdeveloped for his age and he appeared even smaller in his oversized winter jacket and "two sizes, too big" pair of gumboots. He quickly became known for leaving his short, light brown hair uncombed and staring out the car window as if in deep thought, when we drove together during our sessions.

I was informed ahead of time of how shy and timid Daniel was, and how he instinctively withdrew from social situations because of the severe emotional and physical abuse he suffered at the hands of his father. Fortunately, Daniel was removed from harm and placed in the care of a very loving foster family. While under their care, I had the privilege of working with Daniel for 10 hours every 2 weeks.

For the first month or so, a lot of work had to be done to build trust and rapport between the two of us. I paid close attention to the fact that Daniel had major issues with male authority figures, due to the brutal mistreatment he had received from his father, so I put a lot of effort into creating an environment that provided him with an appropriate amount of "safe space." This allowed Daniel to operate at his own pace and helped establish safety, mutual respect, positivity, fairness, and fun throughout our work together.

Although it took a while, Daniel began to soften his stance with me, and he grew increasingly more relaxed and open. In fact, on one of our visits, I even noticed that he took a liking to some of the sporting equipment that was available at one of the parks we visited regularly. He seemed to enjoy bouncing and throwing around some of the balls, namely the basketball.

Knowing Daniel's situation and witnessing some of his behaviours first-hand, I guessed some of his I-am messages to be "I am alone" and "I am helpless." According to *The New Game Plan*, these types of negative messages make it important for Daniel to end up playing pseudo-team or team sports, but for progress to occur, it had to be spurred on by an activity that first guaranteed his safety and comfort. Remember, the type of sport that would help a child who has thoughts, such as "I am alone" and "I am helpless," feel the most safe is the individual sport. That's exactly where we began, but in Daniel's case, a bit of a twist was added.

Although Daniel showed genuine interest in playing with the basketball, this didn't mean that he wanted to play the sport on a team. He made that quite clear when I asked him, so we decided to make up our own individual sport using his new favourite ball, the basketball.

On our next visit, Daniel and I spent the afternoon at a park where there were a number of basketball hoops for us to use. After we became a bit more familiar with our surroundings, I engaged Daniel in a little basketball activity. His task was to throw the ball at the hoop, and if the ball hit any part of the hoop's rim, he would get a point (knowing that actually getting the ball in the hoop would be a difficult task and not a great way of setting him up for success).

Daniel told me he wanted to try and get 10 points on his own, and to create a little more excitement, he suggested that we "time" the whole thing. This "basketball shoot-out" became a part of our routine for the next few weeks. Daniel seemed overjoyed with this new sport which, for all intents and purposes, was an individual sport because of its focus on isolated play. It made complete sense why he enjoyed it so much. The basketball shoot-out gave Daniel the safe space that his negative "I am alone" message required, but it also allowed him to participate in something that reflected his age and skill level. Keep in mind that Daniel only needed to hit the rim of the basketball hoop, which was far less intimidating than actually making a "basket." The activity was designed to help him transform his negative "I am alone" message into a more positive "I am independent" message. The activity also helped Daniel develop an "I am self-reliant" belief to replace his "I am helpless" belief because of the time value and point value attached to the task.

Our fun with the activity didn't end there. As the weeks passed, I noticed that Daniel was actually getting the ball in the hoop more frequently. We decided that hitting the rim would be worth one point and shooting it through the hoop would be worth two. Since the activity would still be "timed," it meant that Daniel could actually have quicker times in the 10-point games that he played by getting more balls in the hoop. I mentioned to a co-worker about my planned objective for Daniel, and he brought along his young male client for a visit with us. Daniel and I had met them before, so inviting them to "our" park and introducing them to the basketball shoot-out wasn't going to be uncomfortable for him. Basically, the same rules were applied and each of the boys performed the game independently. The goal of the activity was to have each of their times added together to see whether or not their combined times could have surpassed the standard we had set before they began. The standard was always set high enough so that they could have actually beaten it, but not so easy as to have made it obvious. Setting up the basketball shoot-out in this way allowed both children to contribute without experiencing the anxiety associated with relying on the other. Combining their individual times was actually a way of making the basketball shoot-out a pseudo-team sport. Remember, a score-combination is a form of indirect interaction (see Chapter 1 on page 23-24).

Over the next couple of months, I scheduled a few more joint visits with my co-worker and his client, and noticed by Daniel's behaviour that he was beginning to believe "I am part of a group," "I am capable," and "I am communicating well with others." Then one day, something extraordinary happened. Daniel, feeling ever so comfortable with his new companion and familiar surroundings, decided on his own to ask his counterpart to do the basketball shoot-out together!

With minimal guidance from us, they turned the basketball shoot-out into a team sport by alternating shots and tracking the amount of time it took for the two of them to reach 20 points as a team.

Within 6 months of our contract, Daniel had made huge progress in his social interactions with others, and according to his foster parents, the lessons he took away from the basketball shoot-out had generalized to other activities and other settings, including the classroom and the playground. If he wasn't getting involved in new activities with other children, he was initiating ideas on his own. Daniel was, quite simply, demonstrating more healthy and productive behaviours than he had ever shown before. This story is just one of many that highlights sport as a major life tool and we'll get a chance to re-visit Daniel's story later on in the final chapter.

<u>Top 7 Signs Of Healthy Self-Esteem</u>

1. Task Initiation: your child initiates new tasks and leads activities with siblings and friends
2. Independent Thinking: your child voluntarily offers opinions and engages in discussions with others
3. Conflict Resolution: your child resolves conflicts and co-operates well with others
4. Effective Communication: your child expresses feelings in the moment
5. Contentment: your child appears pleased with his or her own effort and with life in general
6. Increased Participation: your child is more involved in sports, games, programs, and activities
7. Relationship Building: your child is skilled at making friends at school, in the neighbourhood, on the team, and so forth

<u>Sarina's Super Soccer Success</u>

Daniel's situation shows us how a child can move through all three categories of sport in one direction (from individual to pseudo-team to team sports), but there are many children who benefit from going in the opposite direction (from team to pseudo-team to individual sports). Sarina was one of these children, and she was a regular visitor at the recreation centre at which I supervised. Her bubbly nature made her quite popular amongst the centre's staff and patrons, and she became quite well-known for skipping about the hallways with her blonde pigtails swinging back and forth in the air. At the age of 10, she was the youngest of three girls and was then living in a single-parent home. Her mother revealed to me that Sarina, out of all of her children, was the most devastated when her marriage broke up with Sarina's father. She hinted that the father had been involved in selling and using illegal drugs, and she did not want to see her children growing up in that kind of environment. That's when they decided to pack up their belongings and leave town for good.

Now, Sarina and her mother appeared to have a close relationship but as even her mother admitted, Sarina was in need of some positive male influences in her life. She also expressed great concern about Sarina being too much of a "follower," and she complained that her daughter was unable to complete her homework on her own, copied everything her sisters did, and fought hard not to sleep in her own bed at night. As we often see with youngest children (see pages 150-152 for more information on birth order), they tend to use their cuteness and charm to manipulate others into performing tasks for them; and Sarina might well have been falling into this trap.

At the recreation centre, Sarina often tagged along behind me whenever I watched the kids playing in the gym. When she did participate, it was clear by her lack of confident play that she believed "I am incapable" and "I am in need of others." So in order to help her develop more positive I-am messages, I thought it would make more sense if I met her on her turf which, in this case, was soccer. Sarina absolutely loved playing soccer, and when you think about it, why wouldn't she? It was a sport that gave her a chance to be active while simultaneously allowing her to rely heavily on others, if needed.

From the time that Sarina started coming to the centre, she was a regular at the drop-in soccer program which was offered twice a week for kids her age. This gave me an idea. For the next few months, I thought that I would supervise the program but add a few changes.

For the first few weeks, I led the program with a couple of "fun" drills before the kids got ready for their traditional scrimmage. Although these drills were presented as fun, there was definitely a purpose to them. The first set of drills emphasized indirect interaction to encourage more independent behaviour and develop more positive I-am messages, such as "I am capable." We know that Sarina would feel most comfortable participating in a team sport activity, but since we were scrimmaging (a team activity) later on in the session, the transition to a pseudo-team drill, emphasizing indirect interaction and isolated play, wouldn't be that much of a change for her. In fact, one pseudo-team drill in particular became quite a favourite amongst the entire group. It was called the "breakaway" challenge. This drill pitted the goalkeeper versus the shooters. Basically, if there were 8 shooters, the goalkeeper would have to face 3 shots from each shooter (for a total of 24 shots). The challenge was for the shooters to score a combined amount of goals, also known as a score-combination. In this case, the shooters were challenged to score 10 goals. This drill gave the appearance of a team activity but there was really no direct interaction. It was a safe way for Sarina and the other children to do things independently, such as breakaways, while contributing to the group challenge of scoring 10 goals in total.

The group responded well to these types of drills for the few weeks that we tried them. When I noticed that Sarina and the other participants were becoming really comfortable with these activities, I decided to move them towards more isolated play drills. Over the next month, they were put through a soccer obstacle course that combined the skills they had developed in the previous weeks. The last part of the drop-in hour was dedicated to this obstacle course, which emphasized dribbling, shooting, and passing. The drill took anywhere from 30 to 40 seconds to complete, but the major difference was that there was no score-combination or group task. Instead, individual times were taken. Participants were pretty much competing against each other, making the obstacle course an individual sport. Before we began the drill, I made a point of checking in with Sarina. I reminded her of the skills she had improved upon over the past few weeks, in hopes of lessening any potential anxiousness she might have been experiencing, and then explained to her that all of those skills were involved in the activity she was about to do. By the way in which she did the drill, you wouldn't have noticed any nervousness whatsoever. Even though her time didn't rank anywhere near the top, Sarina participated in an independent activity and completed it with a sense of purpose and efficiency. She didn't stumble, give up, or seem out of place at all.

In the weeks that followed, Sarina's time became very competitive with the others, and she appeared to be a lot more self-assured in her play. This not only impacted Sarina's soccer ability but her interactions throughout the centre. It appeared as though she was beginning to believe "I am self-reliant" and "I am confident," as she grew increasingly more comfortable with individual activities. Staff members were also able to utilize her new-found confidence, and they enlisted Sarina as a centre volunteer. Her help with special events and programs was invaluable. She became someone who could easily be relied upon to complete tasks on her own without any supervision from staff. Sarina's mother also approached me a few months later. She was very pleased with the centre's staff and marveled at the progress her daughter was making. She no longer had to "get after" Sarina about sitting down to do her homework or sleeping alone in her room at night. As my staff attested, Sarina was even developing her own set of friends and didn't follow a step behind her sisters anymore.

With Sarina, we were also able to witness what I like to call the "boomerang effect." Sarina's soccer improvements led to her personal improvements which, in turn, led to more athletic improvements. You see, approximately one and a half years later, with an increased confidence in her abilities, Sarina tried out for the girls' under-13 rep soccer team and was absolutely thrilled when she made it. This type of circular improvement is just another example that highlights sport as a major life tool. Stay tuned to find out more about Sarina in Chapter 6.

Chalk Talk: Using *The New Game Plan* Off The Field

Although *The New Game Plan* focuses on sports, your children may still realize the full benefits of this approach without ever having to play a sport. As in the sporting world, you will still need to make good guesses about your children's I-am messages but, instead, relate them to a breakdown of planned non-athletic activities in terms of direct interaction, communication, and isolated play. For example, in dealing with children who tend to withdraw from social situations, there are several non-athletic activities that would help encourage greater social involvement. For children who are, say, artistic, you may want to start them out in an individual activity that allows them to paint alone, draw alone, or write alone. You can then move them along by organizing pseudo-team activities that allows them to still work alone, but in the context of a group. Later, as their comfort level with pseudo-team exercises increases, you can introduce these children to more team tasks. In short, *The New Game Plan* approach applies to extra-curricular activities in the same way that it does to sports.

As we're finding out, sports may be used to combat the athlete's paradox (see page 11), by helping to build our children's self-esteem. Daniel and Sarina taught us that exposure to more than just one type of sport is the key to creating a healthy balance in life. In other words, by strategically exposing children to all the levels of interaction associated with Social Interest, we are able to increase their belief in their own ability and value. This, you may recall, is the definition of self-esteem. Simply put, *The New Game Plan* gives us a way to ensure, not just hope, that our children become both excellent athletes and excellent people.

EXTRA INNING:
Do Parents Care How Pro Sports Run Their Businesses?

I have to admit that I debated for awhile about whether or not to include this particular "Extra Inning" in the book. I kept asking myself: "Do parents care about how pro sports run their businesses?" Well, after some careful thought, I believe that many of you do, and if you don't, I'm guessing you might think a little bit differently once you've finished reading this section.

Let's begin by first acknowledging the direct impact that pro sports has on our children. For many kids, the dream of playing in the "pros" is as real as the uniforms they wear. Even if our children don't have aspirations of becoming pro athletes, their athletic experiences will still be affected by the professional sporting world. You see, the structure of our children's leagues, the methods used by their coaches, and the ambitions of other parents and players are all shaped by the pro version of the game. And the older our kids get and the higher level of sport they play, the more impacted their athletic environments will be by the professional game.

So you can understand why the business structure

of sport is so important. The professional system needs to be built in such a way that the domino effect of league operations has a positive trickle down impact on our children and their athletic environments. Well-thought out league structures need to be developed so that when pro leagues find themselves in trouble, financial or otherwise, they won't have to resort to tactics that will have a negative influence on the game and, ultimately, our youngsters. Fortunately, the professional sports applications you are about to read, if implemented today, would improve the professional environment and lead to a much healthier experience for our children in the process.

If you recall, in the previous "Extra Inning" I mentioned that *The New Game Plan* can balance payrolls and level the playing field in each of the major professional leagues. It accomplishes this with strategies that encourage a healthy partnership between players and owners, and it ensures league prosperity instead of labour unrest. An unfortunate example of this is in the NHL. In comparison to the other pro leagues, the NHL generates way less revenue than the NFL, the NBA, and MLB. As a result, the NHL's economic issues become much more transparent than their counterparts, forcing this once proud association to become the first professional league to lose an entire season due to a labour dispute. Yes, they ended their crisis, but unfortunately, they did so using an incomplete system that will likely lead to labour unrest again in the future.

Fortunately, a plan has been developed for the NHL using *The New Game Plan* theory, so that the league can operate under a more effective collective bargaining agreement (or CBA). For an in-depth outline of this new system, you can read the book entitled *The New Game Plan - Moving Towards A Common Goal* or visit www.newgameplan.com. Basically, the book uses comprehensive NHL finances and statistics to show that the system actually works, and it uses principles that can be readily applied to other sports and other professional leagues. The plan is designed to prevent future labour disputes and will certainly have an impact on our children, since it is the only plan that integrates direct interaction, communication, and isolated play in its set-up.

Now, the first stage of this new system involves categorizing players. When we categorize players we automatically show respect for every type of player role. The second stage is directly tied to the first stage, and it involves defining these new player categories with game statistics that cover all three forms of Social Interest. This opens the door for the fair rating and ranking of players, which in the sports world is huge. For the first time ever, players could be evaluated using objective criteria.

If leagues adopt these first two stages and accept player categorization along with player rankings, we'll begin to see more balanced play at our children's games. Right now, only one type of player is recognized in sports. In hockey, basketball, and other team sports, the goal-scorers and point-getters receive most of the attention and all of the credit. Not much of the spotlight is put on the other players who perform roles built on hard work and team play. A new system that emphasizes all aspects of the team game and respects all player roles will eventually filter down healthier messages to our kids and teach them to develop more balanced and well-rounded playing habits.

The third and fourth stages of this new system expand upon the first two stages. The third stage attaches player salaries to the player rankings offered in the second stage. When we base player contracts on player performance, we create a fair way to pay players. This takes us to the fourth and final stage, which ties player salaries to the ebbs and flows of league revenue. By linking this entire pool of player money to

the ups and downs of league economics, we guarantee that the total amount of player salaries is exactly
what a pro league can afford.

These last two stages reinforce what the first two
stages do for our kids. The first two stages recognize
all player roles, and the final two stages reward them.
What better way is there for pro leagues to promote
balanced play amongst our youngsters, than to show
them that defensive players and all-round players are
paid just as well as their offensive counterparts?

It wouldn't hurt the NHL and the other professional
leagues to give some serious consideration to this new
type of system. It will not only resolve their immedi-
ate issues, but impact their sport at every level. If any
of the leagues need to be reminded about the importance of grooming well-rounded athletes, just point
them to the headlines at the beginning of this book. In
the next "Extra Inning," we'll take a look at the state of
professional sport from a much different angle.

CHAPTER 3

The Dangers Of Overindulgence

It's becoming quite clear that participation in sports has a profound impact on our children's overall development. But there's another side of sports participation that we need to look at if our kids are to truly benefit from getting involved. I refer to this "other side" as *overindulgence*, and, in understanding the dangers of overindulgence, we can protect our children from falling into the trap of the athlete's paradox. You see, children who overindulge in sports only participate in them to support unhealthy beliefs about themselves. They play for reasons unrelated to having fun, developing skills, or improving themselves.

In the previous chapter, we looked at the positive beliefs that are associated with a healthy approach to sports, but overindulgence in athletics negatively affects these beliefs. Children who play "just to win" instead of "just for fun," or play to "be the best" instead of "do the best they can" develop negative I-must messages in place of positive I-am messages. At one time or another, we've all witnessed children being pushed to play sports in this negative way, but many parents don't realize that this unhealthy approach can literally be life-altering. Since a solid understanding of overindulgence is critical in determining whether or not our children build healthy self-esteem, this entire chapter will be dedicated to exploring the ways in which negative I-must messages develop.

Before we begin our discussion, I should clarify the difference between an I-must message and positive, goal-oriented self-talk. The unproductive "I must always *be the best*" message may look similar to "I must *do my job*," but they differ in a big way. *Be the best* refers to an unattainable goal that is tied to your character. *Do my job* is an attainable goal that reflects the completion of a task and may be related to a positive I-am message such as "I am capable." Simply put, not all self-beliefs containing "I-must" are unhealthy or indicate the negative I-must messages we refer to throughout the book.

A False Sense Of Security:
You Can Hear The Warning Bells

So just how do unhealthy I-must messages develop? Well, they basically stem from the negative version of an I-am message. If "I am inadequate" and "I am worthless," for instance, are held by our children for too long, these negative I-am messages will cause an extreme amount of mental discomfort and lead to unbearable feelings of inferiority. The warning bells inside our children's heads would begin to ring wildly out of control. What are our children to do? If they are stuck holding onto negative I-am messages for too long, they can't just magically transform them into positive I-am messages. Unfortunately, without some healthy strategies or interventions, their negative I-am messages will eventually turn into I-must messages. "I must always be the best" and "I must always win" represent messages that our youngsters might use to protect themselves from experiencing unbearable feelings of inferiority. These new messages give them an artificial sense of superiority, better known as a "false sense of security," which only contributes to poor mental habits and poor coping abilities.

A Peek Into Your Child's Future: Living With I-Must Messages

Wouldn't it be interesting if we could peek into the future to see the impact that our choices could have on us? Well, in a way, we have a chance to peek into our children's futures by examining the difference in the thinking that underlies I-must messages and I-am messages.

Overindulgent children, if you recall, develop I-must messages, and the mindset responsible for this false sense of security is "outcome thinking." Outcome thinking falsely convinces our young kids to focus on results that reflect unattainable ideals. If we were to express these ideals out loud, we would hear something along the lines of "I must always be the best" and "I must always win." It's important to point out that the objective of sports, which is "to win," is not an ideal that reflects this type of outcome thinking message. It actually reflects the goal-oriented self-talk mentioned at the start of this chapter because it is an attainable objective. "I must always win," however, is impossible to do. No one can "always" win, and as you'll see, this ideal has everything to do with a child's character and nothing to do with his or her on-field success. On the surface, an I-must message appears to benefit our children in the short-term, but it only promotes a quick-fix approach that leaves them feeling dissatisfied, frustrated, and unhappy.

Unfortunately, as a culture, we've been taught to believe that outcome thinking will put our children over the top and onto the path of greatness as athletes. But what we don't realize is that this approach psychologically handcuffs our kids. Regardless of what they do on the field, outcome thinking leads to such poor mental habits that their experiences of an event end up being interpreted as negative. Outcome thinkers carry around with them such an idealistic view that they're never satisfied with anything they actually do. A fun round of golf, for instance, will turn sour in the eyes of outcome thinking golfers. After a great shot, they expect to duplicate it every time they swing their club; and after a bad shot, they react aggressively or do a "slow burn" for the entire round. These athletes put so much pressure on themselves to perform that they wind up making more mistakes than they would have otherwise. They become so wrapped up in their own idealistic world that they appear on-edge, come across as unsportsmanlike, and make competition extremely unenjoyable for themselves and those around them.

If we give it some careful thought, how could believing in ideals such as *always* being perfect, *always* winning, and *always* being the best not turn into a negative mindset? Ideals place a lot of pressure on our children every time they step out onto the golf course, ice rink, the tennis court, and so on. We can't expect our kids to achieve an "ideal" because, by definition, it does not exist. It's just that simple. Think of some of the greatest teams or athletes whom you've seen perform. The Chicago Bulls of the 1990's and Tiger Woods come to mind for me. Guess what? They were never *always* perfect nor did they *always* win their games. They didn't even come close to it, yet we seem to think that it's okay for our children to settle for nothing less. Placing such a heavy load on our kids immediately transforms their success into stress because they're being taught to develop an approach that leads to poor coping skills, explosive behaviour, low self-esteem, anxiety, depression, and in many cases, suicidal tendencies. In a nutshell, outcome thinking teaches us to fear failure rather than welcome success.

Outcome thinking is also synonymous with a winning-at-all-costs or "me-first" mentality. Sadly, when both parents and children depend on this approach, the athlete's paradox re-surfaces, and we find ourselves reading all about it in the newspaper. Nowadays, the impact of outcome thinking is fairly easy to spot. It's the athlete who puts individual accomplishments ahead of team success or uses steroids to enhance performance. The warning signs of outcome thinking are all

Top 7 Compulsive Behaviours Of Outcome Thinkers

1. Alcohol Abuse
2. Narcotic or Performance-Enhancing Drug Abuse
3. Excessive Coffee/Caffeine Use
4. Over-Eating
5. Cigarette Smoking
6. Gambling
7. Excessive Computer Use

around us and they offer a sneak peek of what we'll see in our children's future if they live a life shaped by negative I-must messages.

Another Peek Into Your Child's Future: Learning About The "Process"

If you're like most parents, you probably didn't like that earlier glimpse into your child's future through the lens of outcome thinking. Thankfully, an alternative is available to us through a "process thinking" view. Process thinking encourages the development of healthy I-am messages because it focuses on effort and task-completion. Of course, process thinking children care about results too, but not in the same way that outcome thinking children do. Results in the process thinking world do not reflect outcomes tied to your child's character. They instead reflect attainable goals that represent fun, self-improvement, and skill-development. The process thinking child is truly motivated by thinking, "I am doing the best I can," instead of, "I must always be the best." That's why success to process thinkers is ongoing and constant. They are able to view mistakes, not as errors, but as real opportunities from which to learn. They are quite skilled at taking the positive out of any situation.

Does this mean that process thinking children don't get disappointed? Of course not! It's just that their strong coping skills allow disappointment and frustration to subside much quicker than outcome thinkers. They understand the difference between excellence and perfection; and yes, there is a difference between the two. Children who strive for excellence have a great desire and passion to succeed, but never at the expense of the learning process and the development of skills. To them, there is no need for quick-fixes because they enjoy every aspect of participating and competing in their sport. They use an approach that is built on healthy coping strategies, a sense of hard work, open-mindedness, and a positive outlook. Unlike the outcome thinking approach, the process thinking approach leads to both short and long-term success. Believing that "I am doing the best I can" allows a child to ask "self-esteem enhancing" questions, such as: "What did I learn from this experience?" or "How can I continue to improve?" Notice that these questions apply to any situation whether it's a win, a loss, a first place finish, or a last place finish. Ironically, process thinking children who concentrate on learning, task, and effort, instead of perceived mistakes are way more productive on the field. Go figure!

The process thinking approach, also known as the "winning-at-the-*right*-costs" mentality, comes across as being "team-minded" and "hard working." It is the secret to many underdog athletes and less talented teams making it to the finals, such as the Wimbledon Finals or the Stanley Cup Championship. When you meet process thinking athletes, it is very easy to respect them as people. Although task-focused and determined, they are extremely approachable, sportsmanlike, and can appreciate the spirit of healthy competition (which we hinted at on page 22). The success that comes to these athletes is not only well-deserved, it's also bound to happen when you consider that through process thinking, they develop a positive mindset that allows them to tackle the many challenges life has to offer.

Chalk Talk: Routines Or Superstitions?

"Put the left sock on first and the right sock on last." How do you know whether or not this statement represents a routine or a superstition? Well, if athletes use this practice to get organized, focused, and relaxed, then it can be considered a healthy routine based on process thinking. Routines are great mental energy savers. The more automatic things become, the less thought has to go into them. It's sort of like what happens when we drive a car. When we first learn to drive, we really pay attention to turning, reversing, and parking the car, but after a few years, these actions tend to become second nature. The same thing can happen with the "put the left sock on first and the right sock on last" practice. Even if the order is reversed and the right sock went on first, not last, this change wouldn't unsettle the process thinker. If an athlete is thrown off by such a change, it indicates that the practice is used to support outcome thinking. Outcome thinkers will likely attribute special qualities to this practice and give it power or influence over their performance. That's how a practice turns into a superstition.

Can You Feel The Difference?

We've talked a great deal about the messages that our children carry around in their heads, and the profound impact that their beliefs have on their self-esteem. One method I use to highlight this impact is to have audience members say a couple of messages out loud for everyone to hear. Humour me, if you will, and shout out the following message with some emotion and conviction:

"I must be perfect!"

Now, in the same fashion say the following:

"I am doing the best I can!"

You can feel the difference, can't you?

The pressure you put on yourself with the I-must statement is only a hint of what our children experience when they overindulge in athletic activities. When you consider that each of us harbour many more than just one type of message, you can appreciate the importance of developing a positive set of I-am messages.

The Lure Of The Quick-Fix

After understanding both approaches, you may be wondering why some people get themselves caught up in the trap of outcome thinking. Think about it in this way. The psychology attached to outcome thinking is very similar to the psychology attached to people who smoke a pack of cigarettes a day, drink huge quantities of coffee, abuse alcohol, or consume drugs despite knowing the dangers of nicotine, caffeine, alcohol, and dangerous chemical combinations. Millions of people around the world seem to think that they need a quick-fix to soothe unbearable feelings of stress and anxiety, despite knowing that these habits are unhealthy and contribute to their downward spiral. Outcome thinking is no different. It's like a mental drug that gets you by only for the moment, and helps you forget that using it can severely impair your life. It's our job as parents and teachers to make sure that our children stay far away from this quick-fix mentality and, instead, develop a healthy mindset that allows them to overcome life's challenges.

Below, is a sample list of the I-must messages associated with each type of sport arising out of outcome thinking. Compare these messages, which contribute to low self-esteem, with the positive I-am messages promoted through process thinking in Chapter 2 (see page 39):

Team Sports

I <u>must</u> always depend upon others
I <u>must</u> always be the best amongst my peers
I <u>must</u> always prove myself
I <u>must</u> always win

Pseudo-Team Sports

I <u>must</u> always rely on myself
I <u>must</u> always be the best amongst my peers
I <u>must</u> always prove myself
I <u>must</u> always win

Individual Sports

I <u>must</u> always rely on myself
I <u>must</u> always be the best
I <u>must</u> always isolate myself
I <u>must</u> always win

<u>Ref...Time-Out Please!</u>

At the risk of repeating myself, it's important not to lose sight of the reasons why our children play sports. There are so many of us who live vicariously through our children and, in doing so, encourage the development of I-must messages. Fathers, who spend every waking minute of the day preparing their pre-adolescent sons for a career in pro football, and mothers, who sacrifice their family's financial security just for a shot at an Olympic figure skating medal, exist all over North America. If this sounds a bit like you, I strongly encourage you to take this time-out with me and ponder upon some of the following points about your children growing up in high-pressured environments:

- They will play sports to seek your approval.

- They will carry around burdens unfit for a child.

- They will be unable to think for themselves and have difficulty developing their own identities.

- They will be susceptible to using performance-enhancing drugs.

- They will put your needs ahead of their own.

- They will have a difficult time sustaining healthy relationships.

- They will experience more attention and adoration than their siblings.

- They will be unprepared for life if they were to suffer a career-threatening injury.

If any of the above sounds foreign to you, I urge you to stop what you are doing and take a few seconds to visualize your children 10 years from now. Ask yourself, "Are my children equipped to lead a balanced life without me based on what I've taught them up to this moment?" Please don't make the mistake of thinking that your children's problems will go away by them simply becoming professional athletes. If anything, fame and fortune will only magnify their shortcomings.

After reading this book, I encourage you to take the time to access available parenting resources in your area. There are numerous programs, classes, and support networks that can assist you in changing your overall approach. Your children are worth it!

EXTRA INNING:
<u>Sports Biggest Epidemic</u>

Say as much as you want on the topic about using stiffer fines and penalties to curb steroid use, criminal offences, and athlete violence, there is nothing out there that addresses the real problem in sport: individualism. Individualism, as I see it, is the belief that you are more important than others. It's the athlete's paradox, overindulgence, the winning-at-all-costs mentality, and outcome thinking all rolled into one. But, we must not confuse individualism with individual skill or isolated play. They're completely different. Individualism is an approach. Isolated play is an act. Sometimes individualism is expressed through isolated play, but the two are very distinct. Explained in this way, individualism can be considered the biggest epidemic in sports today at every level. Ending its spread, however, requires professional leagues to actually recognize their role in the problem. At this time, I don't think they're ready to do so. I don't know whether or not pro leagues realize the types of messages they send out to the entire sporting community, and if they shrug off their responsibility, it will only come back to haunt them. Who do they think listens to the messages they put out there? Their future athletes, of course. Furthermore, if leagues fool themselves into believing that these athletes aren't going to mimic what's already being done, they're in for a rude awakening.

In the previous "Extra Inning," we highlighted the importance of collective bargaining agreements, and we'll continue to highlight it here, but from a much different angle. As we discussed before, a well-outlined CBA affects the structure of an entire sport, and to not give it careful thought, or to assume that it is "only" a financial application limits its use. Traditionally, this has been the case. Without a well-designed CBA, our hopes of eliminating individualism diminish greatly. Unfortunately, every professional league is governed by an underdeveloped CBA that targets only the financial aspects of the game. This wouldn't be a bad thing if the financial systems that flowed from these CBA's were designed to have a positive impact on players. Despite the important relevance of our recommendations in the last "Extra Inning," the reality is that only a few types of athletes get handsomely rewarded. You may say, "big deal," but it is! When certain players are rewarded significantly more than other players, without any objective reason, leagues are saying, without literally saying it, that some roles are more important than others. This reinforces individualism.

Think about it for a moment. Imagine you're a top-notch 8-year veteran linebacker in the NFL. You put your heart and soul into every game you play by doing all the little things that your team needs you to do in order to have a shot at the Super Bowl. Now, imagine you get paid "half" as much as a star rookie wide receiver who has played in only half the number of games that you have played and, gave half-hearted efforts in each of them. Would you be bitter? Many players would be. Any CBA that allows this to happen doesn't show respect for the different roles that exist on a team and can be considered severely flawed. Just ask the many clubs out there, whose on-field success depends heavily on contributions from their non-star players, about the importance of each player's role.

Unfortunately, the blatant lack of respect associated with the way in which player salaries are distributed ends up filtering down to our future pros. The message becomes loud and clear to these young up-and-comers, and to those who train them, that professional sports rewards individualism, and in order to make it to the big leagues, these youngsters need to develop this harmful mindset.

You and I both know that there are parents out there who believe that their children are the next "big things" in sports, and they use the highest paid athletes as a frame of reference. They may refer to Vince Carter in basketball, Sergei Fedorov in hockey, and Ken Griffey Jr. in baseball as athletes whom their children should look up to and admire. These pros, without a doubt, are highly skilled, but not too many of them belong on playoff teams. Even if they have made it to the post-season, they aren't very well known for their playoff exploits. What does this tell you? Well, it tells me that professional sport focuses on just one aspect of the game when they pay players. These leagues need to realize that it's not all about isolated play or scoring points. They have to give some serious thought to the stuff that leads up to goals being scored, baskets being made, and touchdowns being caught. A hockey player winning an important face-off, a basketball player grabbing a key rebound, or a football player diving to make a block are all important steps leading up to a score. Unfortunately, the only time these plays get the recognition they deserve is in the playoffs.

Playoff success is one of the biggest thrills an athlete can experience. It's that time of the sports year when participation becomes more about the game than about the paycheck. All individual accolades are put aside, and players willingly contribute in any way they can to help their club reach the big game. But when it's all said and done, who gets rewarded the following season? It's not the defensive player that blocks 4 shots a game or the leading scorer that sacrifices some of his offence to create more chances for his teammates. No, we reward the players that we gave mention to earlier - the ones with lots of goals and assists on a last place team that didn't even make it to the post-season. Unbelievable! If we allow this to continue, individualism will run rampant, and we'll witness the demise of professional sports, first-hand.

Before I'm accused of not wanting to encourage skill in sports, think again. As I said earlier, I'm addressing a mindset not a talent. I applaud players who have the rare ability to bring the fans out of their seats with dashing speed, electrifying moves, and other exciting forms of isolated play. But, I give a standing ovation to the players who are team-oriented and are playing in leagues governed by economic systems that do not support them. They are truly the amazing ones, and something has to be done so that they become the rule, not the exception.

Individualism also explains why apathy is experienced on the part of sports fans. Fans just don't seem to be as connected to their favourite athletes the way they once were. Do you really expect today's superstars, raised in a culture of individualism, to spend time signing autographs or speaking to long-time supporters? When you factor in that the price of tickets for a family of four to a big league sporting event may cost as much as a plane ticket to your favourite vacation spot, you'll sympathize with fans who feel they're being ripped-off and pushed away from the game they love. Corporate sports leagues need to also realize that they're making it difficult for the younger generation to care. We're talking about their future consumers. Not too many of them can afford $100 for tickets to watch their favourite teams in action.

Finally, individualism is the main reason why youngsters get caught up in the athlete's paradox and behave so inappropriately. Children who believe they are more important than others (which we know indicates a false sense of security) will resort to cheating with banned substances and use violence in an attempt to prove their perceived elite status. Unfortunately, they can't change this behaviour in the real world with the flick of an "off switch." That's why, whenever we turn on the sports channel, there's a good chance we'll see athletes on a witness stand or in handcuffs instead of on the ice, the basketball court, the football field, or the baseball diamond where they belong.

Fortunately, not all is doom and gloom. As we showed in the previous "Extra Inning," a system can be tailor-made to any league to replace any CBA. This system respects all player roles, ranks their performances using objective criteria, and pays them fairly based on performance. I don't think players, owners, or fans will have much of a problem with athletes receiving big contracts based on merit, and the domino effect of a multi-faceted pay structure throughout the sporting world would trigger the end of individualism as we know it. But the question still remains, "Are the leagues ready to accept their part in it all?" We can only hope.

CHAPTER 4

The Deadly Impact Of Our Thoughts

With the first three chapters under our belts, we are in a much better position to prevent the headlines mentioned at the start of the book from occurring. Stories of athletes involved in murder plots, scandals, and criminal trials are sobering reminders of the deadly impact of our thoughts on our behaviours. Now, I'll be the first to admit that athletes need to take responsibility for the headlines they create, but to end our discussion here wouldn't paint a complete picture. As a culture, we have to share some of the blame. When we consider that sports, businesses, families, and schools are aspects of the community built on years and years of outcome thinking, it shouldn't come as a shock to us when our children adopt this very approach. We bombard our children with such an overwhelming amount of parenting, coaching, and teaching styles based on this negative mindset that they are bound to experience its detrimental effects. If our children answered honestly when asked about their feelings about life in general, a large percentage of them would reveal their unbearable stress and deep sense of despair. If you think I'm off base, think again! The second leading cause of death in Canada and the third leading cause of death in the United States, amongst 15 to 24 year olds, is suicide. We can't afford to ignore this harsh truth. I couldn't even imagine any of my nieces or nephews considering suicide as an option. It breaks my heart to even think about it, let alone write it down in this book. Sadly, suicide has become a cruel reality for many families who have to deal with the immense pain it brings them every day.

Before suicide occurs, there are many outward indicators, including alcohol abuse, drug use, steroid consumption, and a host of other unhealthy quick-fixes that warn us a child's stress level is unbearably high. Grateful as I am to be in a profession that allows me to battle this issue, we all need to work together to ensure a more promising future for our kids. One athlete we can learn from is Phil. After reading his story, you'll witness first-hand the influence of a young athlete's self-beliefs. Since Phil's story goes into greater depth than the other stories do, you'll be exposed to more of the learning process and pick up some helpful teaching tools along the way.

Phil "The Thrill"

"You suck! Get off the ice! Why are you even playing?" Phil yelled in disgust. Harsh words, you might say, from a 16 year-old hockey player, but even harsher when you consider that his crude remarks were reserved for an already dejected teammate. I quickly began to understand why his mom, dad, and coaches were concerned. Despite Phil being highly sought after by scouts from higher level junior teams, Phil's family and coaches felt that his attitude was poor and would interfere with his ability to play hockey at the next level. They strongly believed that some sort of intervention was needed and invited me, with Phil's permission, to watch him play at a tournament.

In the four games I saw at the tourney, Phil's behaviour was embarrassing to say the least. He continually slashed his stick against the glass in frustration and swore profusely at his opponents. His blatant overindulgence in the game was affecting his play and the overall morale of his team. In the third game of the tourney, after scoring into an empty net, he celebrated by riding his hockey stick like a broom and then proceeded to taunt the other team by chanting, "Phil-The-Thrill-Is-In-The-House!" Later, in the final game, Phil did the unthinkable. After his club gave up a late goal in the third period, he pushed his very own teammate down to the ice in frustration. I knew I had my work cut out for me, if we decided to work together.

Getting To Know "The Thrill"

After watching Phil's performance at the tournament, I scheduled a meeting just between the two of us. I was interested in working with him as a client, but we first needed to meet one-on-one to see whether we could establish some kind of rapport. We met after a team practice and discussed my possible role in his training. Phil seemed pretty "cool" with my involvement and indicated that he knew what I did for a living. He had heard from some of his friends, who played on other teams, about the improvements they had made through the work we had done together. I made a point of emphasizing the "together" part of his comment to set the stage for our possible work with each other. We discussed that my approach would not only allow him to learn from me, but allow me to learn from him. My guess was that even though Phil played a team sport, he rarely demonstrated the qualities of being a team player, so instilling the team concept immediately, even in such a subtle way, was essential at this stage of our rapport building.

Moments later, I asked Phil whether he understood the reason why I was considering getting involved in his hockey career. He acknowledged that his teammates, coaches, and parents weren't pleased with his attitude. We explored this a little further. He was well aware of their frustration with his on-ice antics, but he easily justified his behaviour by suggesting that he was the star of the team. That's why he nicknamed himself, "The Thrill." He thought of himself as the most electrifying player on the team, and believing this to be true, he felt that he should be able to do whatever he wanted to on the ice.

At this point, I believed that Phil and I could, in fact, work together and agreed to take him on as a client. We discussed that our work could take anywhere from 2 to 6 months, and it would involve us meeting at least twice a week. After Phil agreed to these terms, we entered into a verbal contract (which we communicated later that evening to his parents and coaches), and then continued on with our discussion.

It's All About Goals, But What Type?

After agreeing to our working arrangements, we proceeded to discuss the "goals" of our sessions. Phil didn't seem to have a problem in telling me that his personal goals were to win a scoring championship and become drafted by a junior club, but he was a bit tongue-tied when I asked him about his goals for the team.

Whenever you work with athletes (or any client for that matter), it's imperative that your goals are aligned with theirs. If they aren't, then both parties will end up pulling in different directions and battle each other to get their respective needs met. Aligning goals is the ultimate test of collaboration and sets the stage for becoming a partnership or a team. So, how did I go about aligning my goals with Phil's, which were self-focused and lacking in team-mindedness? Well, I chose my words extremely carefully, keeping in mind that we were in the early phase of developing a working relationship. I suggested that we work together to *help him develop the tools he needed to take his game to the next level.* In Phil's mind, this suggestion was compatible with his goal, and in my mind, it would allow room for Phil to grow in areas such as team-mindedness.

After we had agreed to this as our goal, I immediately inquired about his opinion on what he thought the junior
teams would be looking for in the upcoming player draft.
With great excitement, he replied, "Goals, lots of goals." I
then threw a bit of a verbal wrench at him, "If the junior
clubs who are interested in you have 2 spots to fill and 10
scoring champions to choose from, what do you think
they'll look for, *besides* goal-scoring, when making their
decisions?" He thought about it for a few seconds and
seemed almost dumbfounded that there were other aspects to the game of hockey. He sat in silence for a while
before I asked, "What did your team need to do to score
more in the last tournament?" By focussing on the process of scoring goals, this question was intended to trigger
a different focus. Although it took him some time, Phil
ended up naming, "hard work," "better passing," "a better
fore-check," "better break-outs," and so on; but our conversation didn't end there. We quickly reflected on his play
at the last tournament, and Phil was asked to think of the
times in those games that he had done any of the things
he had just listed. Phil sheepishly looked to the floor and
admitted that he couldn't think of any. Our discussion
about all-round play was sinking in a bit. And to drive the
message home, I added that the more complete a player
he is on the ice, the more likely he would be picked by

a junior club, and the more helpful he would be to his own team. Through these types of conversations, Phil was beginning to realize that his individual goals were closely linked to his goals for the team.

As we saw with Daniel and Sarina, Phil also needed to use his sport to help him become more well-rounded, as well as participate in it in ways that did not make him feel uncomfortable. By coordinating his individual interests with his team's interests, we were in a good position to offset his overdeveloped need for individual success with his underdeveloped need for team success. Come to think of it, creating a healthy balance between the two is the definition of Social Interest, isn't it?

I should point out that I took that particular route with Phil for a couple of reasons. First, if I pushed Phil to be a "team player" at the beginning of our work together, he would have resisted since the concept was too unfamiliar to him when we first met. Second, if Phil felt that I was forcing him to go in a specific direction, it may have indicated to him that his individual goals weren't being considered and that I had no intention of aligning myself with them. Such a perceived lack of respect would have done nothing to create the healthy rapport and positive alliance that was necessary for our sessions to inspire personal growth.

Sports Psychology Vs. Sports Counselling: The Difference Is Personal

The rest of our after-practice meeting outlined the structure that our sessions would take. We ended up scheduling two types of training: skill-development training and mental training. For the skill-development training, I would be on the ice with Phil and his teammates as part of their on-ice practices, and then, for the mental training, we'd meet regularly in my office. Even if Phil didn't realize it at the time, both types of training would help him establish the balance he needed, which is key in developing Social Interest.

The majority of the skill-development training, as mentioned, occurred at Phil's regularly scheduled team practices. Before each practice, I consulted with his coaches, and we designed drills that encouraged Phil and the rest of the team to develop more aspects of the game. If you recall, in Daniel's story, Daniel started with an individual sport because his negative "I am alone" message was supported by isolated play. Remember, isolated play isn't unhealthy, but a child's overindulgent use of it can be.

Phil's situation, however, is a little bit different from Daniel's because of his already developed false sense of security. In Phil's case, his negative I-am messages, which may have included "I am inadequate" and "I am alone," inspired feelings of inferiority too overwhelming to bear. So, as a defensive reaction, these messages instantly transformed into an unhealthy "I must always be the best" type of message, representing his false sense of security. Isolated play actually presented Phil with a way to show off this false sense. As we know, isolated play is a form of interaction that occurs in every type of sport. This meant that Phil could display his false sense of security in any sport. In Phil's eyes, the isolated play found in all sports gave him a chance to prove to others that he was the best. The fact that his two favourite sports were hockey and tennis only confirmed this point. Phil chose hockey because he enjoyed scoring goals, and he played tennis because he thrived on "crushing" his opponents, both of these being very overindulgent uses of isolated play.

When children focus only on isolated play, they end up treating every sport as if it were an individual sport. How could we not expect problems to occur, especially when the sport being played is a team game? Name any player, on any team, who wants to feel inferior to another, be yelled at, or be treated as an opponent is treated. This isn't what working together towards a common goal is supposed to look like.

As indicated, Phil's coaches and I put together some practice drills to help Phil and his teammates learn the different aspects of hockey. I had a previous working relationship with both coaches, so we knew what to expect from each other. They were quite comfortable dedicating a segment of their practices to these drills, some of which reversed the roles the players were used to playing in order to develop other skills. For example, we placed Phil and the other forwards on defence in some of the scrimmages and instructed them to start team break-outs, play more defensively, and set-up plays. They were not allowed to score. The regular defencemen were then placed up at the forward positions and instructed to do the opposite. They were encouraged to establish forechecks and score as many times as possible. Drills similar to this one went on for the entire season, teaching each player the importance of all aspects of the game. Having players on a team pay attention to direct interaction, communication, and isolated play, regardless of their positions on the ice, could only improve their overall play.

Now, the mental training sessions were just as important as the skill-development training sessions. But before beginning the mental training with Phil, I took the time to discuss the difference between sports psychology and sports counselling. Sports psychology, I explained, deals with "sport-specific issues" related to the physical skills of the game and is geared primarily towards improving an athlete's performance. I reviewed, with Phil, some of the visualization techniques and stress management strategies used in sports psychology, and indicated that many athletes usually seek out this type of mental training without realizing the benefits of sports counselling.

Sports counselling addresses both "sport-specific issues" and "personal issues." The two, as you already know, go hand-in-hand. All those reports of murder plots, scandals, and criminal trials are disturbing reminders that athletes not only believe they are above everyone else in the sporting world, but "above the law" in the real world too. Sports counselling, fortunately, addresses this vicious cycle. It's a field that understands that personal issues affect athletic issues, and athletic issues in return affect personal issues. We saw this boomerang effect with Sarina. She was able to use sports to her personal benefit and then use her personal improvements to impact her sports participation later on.

The Behaviour Triad:
Connecting Our Thoughts, Feelings,
And Behaviours

The sports counselling sessions scheduled between Phil and I took place weekly at my office. Our first session together allowed me to gather some personal information from Phil and enabled him to get acquainted with the facility. In our second session, Phil gave his approval to invite his parents to attend, so that they could be a part of the process and support any changes or learning that occurred. This, again, emphasized the team approach that we had established at the beginning of our work together.

We began this meeting by exploring Phil's most recent sporting experiences. He revealed that he placed a lot of pressure on himself to perform, and that his "I must always be the best" mentality was the only way he knew how to play. Phil didn't settle for anything other than being better than everyone else, including his very own players. He was driven to score the most goals, get the most points, and win scoring titles. From the start of our work together, Phil adamantly expressed his desire, on many occasions, to be the best, so I took the opportunity to plug his verbalized I-must message into the "behaviour triad." The behaviour triad outlines the connection that exists between thoughts, feelings, and behaviours. In the counselling world, it's understood that thoughts give rise to feelings, which lead to behaviours, which then reinforce thoughts, and so the cycle continues. Graphically, it would look like this:

$$\downarrow \qquad\qquad\qquad\qquad\qquad\qquad \uparrow$$
$$\text{Thoughts} \rightarrow \text{Feelings} \rightarrow \text{Behaviours}$$

In the office, Phil was asked to grab a felt marker and proceed to the flip chart at the end of the room. He drew the behaviour triad and underneath the word "Thoughts," wrote down his belief, "I must always be the best." We agreed that he would ignore, for the next few minutes anyway, that this was "his" thought, so that he could look at it a little more objectively. Phil was asked to jot down on the chart the "Feelings" to which this thought might contribute. He contemplated his answer before I prodded him further with this question: "If someone always needed to prove him or herself, how would this person feel?" As Phil wrote down his answers, you could tell by the concentration shown on his face that this type of exploration was making a huge impression on him. He carefully wrote feeling "stressed out," "on-edge," and "dissatisfied." His mom and dad were respectful of the fact that it was Phil's process and eagerly awaited each of Phil's written responses, which also included a fear of failing, burnout, and frustration.

Our work didn't end there. We still needed to focus on the third part of the triad, which was "Behaviours." I asked Phil, "How would someone react to the feelings listed on the chart?" This was a little more eye-opening and time consuming for him, and quite bluntly, it should have been. When you begin to get insight into yourself, it can be humbling, especially if you thought you had it all figured out. With every response to this section, Phil visibly showed the impact that each was having on him in the moment. I commended him for being so willing to explore his behaviours, which he listed as being "aggressive," "quick-tempered," and "arrogant." A summary of Phil's base thoughts, feelings, and behaviours arising out of his outcome thinking mindset is outlined below:

Phil's Outcome Thinking Base Behaviour Triad

Thought: I must always be the best

Feelings: stress, anxiety, dissatisfaction, anger, isolation, depression, burn-out, on-edge, frustration, failure, rejection, despair, hopelessness

Behaviours: aggressive, abuses substances, avoids others, quick-tempered, suicidal tendencies, cheats, defensive, arrogant, nicknames himself "Phil-The-Thrill"

Top 7 Signs Of Outcome Thinking Athletes

1. They must prove they are better than everyone else
2. They will attempt to change the rules/situation to suit themselves
3. They will show how visibly upset they are about losing
4. They will focus on isolated play while playing team/pseudo-team sports or prefer to participate in individual sports
5. They are superstitious
6. They are unsportsmanlike
7. They have difficulty taking instruction or receiving coaching

When Sports Mirrors Life...

We turned to the flip chart paper in front of us and took some time to discuss the "base" triad that represented Phil's typical thoughts, feelings, and behaviours. We then reflected on some of his recent tournament experiences. We were about to see the connection between the hockey tournament fiasco and his winning-at-all-costs mentality. In the tournament, Phil's team made it to the finals but they lost. In fact, they were shut-out and scored no goals, so I inquired of him, "How did this impact you?" We knew his thought was "I must always be the best," and after losing in the championship final, we needed to explore the state of his feelings in the moment of losing. Phil expressed feeling frustration, disappointment, a sense of failure, anger, and discouragement by the loss. We then moved on to his behaviours. Phil agreed that he was unsportsmanlike and that he shouted and swore uncontrollably. Here is a summary of the entire trigger experience:

Phil's Outcome Thinking Trigger Experience: Losing In The Finals

Thought: I must always be the best

Feelings: anger, disappointment, frustration, failure, insignificance, discouragement

Behaviours: verbal outbursts, slow burns, shouting, recoiling, tantrums, being unsportsmanlike, swearing, acting hurt, acting upset, pushing teammates

Everyone in the room noticed that Phil's written expression of his "trigger" experience was similar to that of his base triad. Phil was realizing that when his current circumstances in life mirrored his base approach, his base approach would only become stronger. In that moment, Phil recognized the connection that his trigger experience had in his personal life. He shyly admitted to binge-drinking with his buddies on a few occasions, as well as feeling a constant high level of stress. He revealed that in the past he had fleeting thoughts of suicide, but reassured us, through a suicidal risk assessment which I conducted in the office, that he was no longer at risk. Phil also admitted to numerous verbal outbursts in his personal life, which actually put a strain on his relationship with his girlfriend. Phil was beginning to understand that if he weren't willing to change his unproductive approach, such a mindset could really impair him. It was becoming clear that if he continued to have experiences similar to the hockey tournament disaster (the trigger), his outcome thinking mindset (the base) would become harder to break.

The entire group realized that outcome thinking emphasized nothing but unattainable goals and ideals. In Phil's case, when his ideals weren't being realized, his approach forced him to view his experiences as failures. As we know, this double-edged sword is common amongst outcome thinkers. They strive for things that are unattainable, and, when they don't attain them, they beat themselves up for their apparent failures. They focus on mistakes so much so that even favourable results are devalued. As we also know, when outcome thinkers pay attention to perceived mistakes, they end up making more of them. Eventually, these athletes who hold a rigid "I must always be the best" message will develop an equally rigid fear of failure, rejection, and isolation.

Chalk Talk: First-Place Fixation

The concept of "first-place fixation" affects many athletes, and it develops from outcome thinking. If Phil, before we did any work together, had won a scoring championship, it would have appeared to him, on the surface, that his "I must always be the best" conviction was justified. Unfortunately, winning the scoring championship would have negatively affected him in two ways. First, his "I must always win" message or "I must always be the best" message would have strengthened. This may have falsely convinced Phil to view first place as a "right" that belonged to him, rather than a privilege or objective that could have been pursued by anyone. Such a mistaken sense of entitlement, along with the increased difficulty of duplicating a scoring championship, would have led to greater feelings of failure, rejection, and isolation, if Phil could not have attained the results that he believed he "owned." Second, the strengthening of Phil's I-must message, because of the winning of his scoring championship, would have lead him to focus more on mistakes. We know that honing in on mistakes leads athletes to make even more of them. With first-place fixation, the margin for error tightens even more, and athletes, such as Phil, end up paying increased attention to what they are doing "wrong," instead of what they are doing "right." Basically, first-place fixation is an extension of outcome thinking, and it leads to severe psychological impairments, unless the athlete is able to counteract it with more effective process thinking strategies.

A Few Light Bulb Moments

In the latter half of our sports counselling session, Phil and his folks were attentively awaiting some solutions to Phil's apparent issues. If he was going to accept process thinking as an alternative, this was the time. Since the previous exploration of the behaviour triad was so effective, we decided to do it again, but this time, we used the alternative to Phil's outcome thinking triads. Underneath the triad headings of Thoughts-Feelings-Behaviours, Phil wrote down the process thinking thought, "I am doing the best I can." In exploring this alternative base thought, we came up with the following:

Phil's "Possible" Process Thinking Base Behaviour Triad

Thought: I am doing the best I can

Feelings: contentment, relaxation, fun, satisfaction, excitement, confidence, courageousness, passion

Behaviours: open-minded, approachable, co-operative, hard working, risk taking, sportsman-like, flexible, competitive, fair play

Phil's insight was continuing to grow. He admitted that he never would have guessed that this approach would work. He simply assumed that athletes who used this approach were "losers" who weren't driven. He was shocked to realize that it was actually his approach that was getting in the way, and that process thinking would allow him to perform better. We also discussed that outcome thinking athletes are guilty of wanting to control outside influences such as referees, the crowd, the field conditions, and all the factors that affect the result of a game. To this, his dad remarked, "No wonder they're so uptight." We pointed out that process thinking athletes, on the other hand, understand that the only thing they are able to control during a game is their own performance. They feel less pressure and are successful because they truly, not superficially, believe that they are doing the best they can.

To end the behaviour triad process, we decided to take a second look at the trigger event of losing in the finals of the hockey tournament. This time around, we plugged in a possible process thinking approach and came up with the following:

Phil's "Possible" Process Thinking Trigger Experience: Losing In The Finals

Thought: I am doing the best I can

Feelings: mild disappointment, mild frustration, satisfaction with effort, appreciation for the opportunity, enjoyment of participation

Behaviours: respectful of opponent, remains relaxed, acknowledges effort, focuses on the positive, learns from experience, laughs it off

The astonishment on Phil's face and the faces of his parents was now at its peak. We reiterated that some of the most successful athletes in the world were those who did not base their athletic existence on success. They actually learn how to go with the flow and deal with things as they naturally occur.

Unlike the outcome thinking triads, the trigger experience of losing in the finals would've become a positive experience for Phil, if he had used a more process thinking approach. In fact, the trigger experience closely resembles the "possible" process thinking base behaviour triad shown earlier.

Remember, there is a circular connection between an athlete's present experience and his or her base approach. The present experience reinforces the base approach, and the base approach returns the favour by shaping the present experience. In Phil's case, a more process thinking set of thoughts, feelings, and behaviours would have led to his present experiences becoming more positive, and these healthier experiences would then have strengthened his newly adopted process thinking approach.

What seemed to make a difference to everyone in the room was the realization that process thinking athletes experience disappointment too. It was just that their perspectives help them cope better with challenging situations. The intention in using the behaviour triad was not to paint a black and white picture and suggest that Phil would never experience negative emotions. Rather, the purpose was to show him how he could deal with negative emotions more effectively through a process thinking approach. That's why the experience of disappointment is mild, not devastating, in the previous process thinking triad. How could athletes not improve with this type of mindset?

It was at this point in our session that Phil was introduced to the exercise you did earlier. He willingly yelled out, "I must always be the best," and then followed it seconds later with, "I am doing the best I can." We all felt the difference, and I mentioned that the change he had just experienced from doing the exercise would take some time and effort, if he wanted to instill it long term. Phil enthusiastically nodded his approval.

Moments later, we took some time to acknowledge that feelings are used to fuel our behaviours (that's why "Feelings" come before "Behaviours" in the behaviour triad). So, in order for Phil to remove feeling "on-edge" and "stressed-out" in a vain attempt to prove that he was the best, we decided to do some relaxation work in the office. This was done to instill more positive emotions in support of the process thinking changes Phil was willing to make to his behaviour. Phil agreed to do these relaxation exercises before every practice and every game, so that he could associate feeling comfortable with the new positive behaviours he was ready to display on the ice.

We then looked back at the "goal" of our sessions, which was to *help him develop the tools he needed to take his game to the next level.* You could see that this goal, at that moment, meant something completely different to him.

At the end of our meeting, Phil's mom and dad thanked me, as did Phil, for the session. I also thanked them and shared my appreciation for their willingness to explore new concepts and be open to a new approach. We agreed that the group's continued collaboration could only spur on greater learning as we worked towards our goal.

Both parents went on to rave about the behaviour triads, process thinking, and other session topics. At one point in the conversation, Phil's mom brought up "success" and what it meant to her. Here's what she had to say: "As a parent, I knew success wasn't about scoring goals and becoming a scoring champion. I think that I just needed to hear it in the way it was said today. To me, it's more about accepting whatever life gives you and then making the most out of it for yourself and those around you. If my son can do this, he'll be a success." I agreed wholeheartedly. Success isn't about fame, riches, prestige, or achievement. Deep down, many of us may want these things for our children because they appear to guarantee security. But, as this entire book shows, there is no greater guarantee for our children's security than a positive approach to life. All that this group had to do was look at the flip chart for proof.

EXTRA INNING:
Is The NBA Finally Getting It?

I have to congratulate the NBA. Their MVP selection for 2005 and 2006 was one of the most dynamic athletes in pro sports today - Steve Nash. Mr. Nash is the consummate team player and his style of play will undoubtedly have a positive impact on the sport right across North America. He has re-introduced "team-ball" or team play to basketball and has, in a sense, brought the sport back to itself. Basketball has long been known for its dunks and other awesome individual displays of athleticism, but the game offers way more than that. As you know, it's about direct interaction, communication, and isolated play. Nash's game is built on all of these aspects. His passing ability and assist average (direct interaction) are unmatched; his leadership (communication) is unparalleled; and his ability to make baskets (isolated play) is unquestioned. I assure you that I have not yet had the pleasure of meeting Mr. Nash, but his well-roundedness as an athlete is hard not to notice.

With the NBA serving as the home to some of the world's most dominant athletes in sport (Shaquille O'Neal quickly comes to mind), its selection of Steve Nash as MVP means *that* much more. Is this world-renowned league beginning to understand that being a "dominant athlete" doesn't necessarily mean being a "team player"? I hope so.

Now, despite the Steve Nash selection, I must admit that I have a huge problem with the MVP award. It is one of the most damaging things in team sports today, and by handing it out at the amateur and pro levels, we are unwittingly rewarding only one part of the game. Let me ask you this, when we traditionally give out this award, who do we give it to? Usually, it goes to the young hockey player who scores the most goals, the football player with the most touchdowns, and the baseball player with the most home runs. Again, we tend to just focus on isolated play. What about giving it to the player who does everything well in the game? Let's stop making well-balanced athletes feel like second-class citizens.

Here's a suggestion: why don't we just get rid of the MVP award all together? It really doesn't represent what team sports are about. I think players, such as Nash, may agree. As honored as Steve Nash may have been to accept the award, he deflected the accolades and admiration he received onto his teammates, where it also belonged. He is one of the rare recipients of the MVP award to bring his teammates onto the podium during his 2005 acceptance speech - a definite show of team-mindedness. He understands that one player cannot do it alone. If the NBA and other leagues decide not to eliminate the award, they could at least change the name of it to the "MVTP Award" (the Most Valuable Team Player Award). This would be a great honor to team-oriented players as long as the award is based on objective criteria that focuses on every level of interaction. Anything short of this is a vote in favour of individualism, and it gives athletes a reason to act as though they are more important than their fellow teammates. We've seen the damage that such a me-first mentality can cause. It's about time that we get back to the team-first approach on which the game was built, and the NBA's acknowledgement of Steve Nash is definitely a step in the right direction.

CHAPTER 5

Choosing Our Words Carefully

Now that we've seen the impact that sports can have on our children's overall development, how do we go about ensuring that our kids get the most out of their sporting careers right from the get go? Well, the answer is as simple as the words we choose to speak. Yes, the difference between children becoming outcome thinkers or process thinkers is as subtle as the language we use.

The Trouble With Being A "Good Girl"

"Good girl, you scored three goals" is a typical statement we might make when complimenting a child. But, there's a big problem with complimenting children in this way. Even though our intentions may be good, the opening statement is a form of praise that focuses on the person and may prove damaging over time. Here's what I mean. After hearing the previous statement, the young girl is likely to ask herself, "Am I still a good girl if I don't score goals?" Once standards and benchmarks become tied to her character, she'll form unhealthy I-must messages, such as "I must always be the best" or, in this case, "I must always score goals." And we know how ineffective these messages are.

Does this mean that praise is a bad thing? No, not at all. It's only detrimental when it's linked to a result. If, out of the blue, you were to say, "You're such a good girl," without attaching this comment to an event, outcome, or occurrence, then it would have a positive impact because you're acknowledging a person's character without tying it to any conditions.

Encouragement, on the other hand, emphasizes behaviour. "Blakey, you played really well," or "You worked hard out there," are encouraging remarks that focus on the process, not the outcome. Even if Blakey didn't play well, he could still be encouraged if I were to simply ask, "How did you feel out there today?" And then offer him feedback and focus on his strengths whenever it was appropriate to do so. With this approach, children would be shown respect at all times and would not have to deal with our adult evaluations thrusted upon them. Their positive I-am messages would also become strengthened because encouragement focuses on the fun and skill-development aspects of a sport.

Simply put, praise focuses on the person, while encouragement focuses on the behaviour. To use some analogies, if praise acknowledges the "runner," encouragement acknowledges the "race." If praise is for the "doer," encouragement is for the "deed." The distinction between the two cannot be overstated. It could mean the difference between your child learning ineffective life-coping strategies, or effective ways of dealing with life's challenges through Social Interest.

It's also important for parents, coaches, and teachers to remember to model the behaviours they hope to instill in their kids. There are so many unfortunate real life occurrences of parents engaging in verbal and physical confrontations with other parents, coaches, and referees, with some altercations even resulting in death. This isn't a laughing matter. Regardless of the reasoning, this sort of behaviour is inexcusable (and will be addressed in the next "Extra Inning"). Children cannot be expected to develop healthy I-am messages when adults model behaviours that run counter to them.

The Power Of "Slushees"

How many of you buy a treat – say *slushees* – for your kids to reward them when they score points, or give them money for doing chores? If you understand the distinction between encouragement and praise, you'll realize that these external rewards are forms of praise. What we're saying to our children when we buy them a slushee after they score is, "Good boy or good girl you scored!" Now, I'm not saying that it's unhealthy to give rewards, it's just the way in which we structure their distribution that is sometimes inappropriate. There's nothing wrong with buying a slushee, as long as it encourages internal motivation instead of external motivation. Internal motivation encourages our children to do something for the sake of the event or the activity. External motivation forces them to get involved in the event because of outside incentives such as prizes, money, and so forth. Internal motivation is born out of Social Interest and process thinking. External motivation is created from outcome thinking. Fortunately, external motivation can shift to internal motivation, and the next story highlights some ways in which this may be done.

A Coaching Story

A couple of years ago, I had the privilege of co-coaching a group of 12-year old boys in soccer. I had known many of them from just being around the game and around the soccer community, so I was well aware of the team that the other coach and I were going to inherit. For the most part, the boys were extremely talented, but were very individualistic in their play. They seemed to have no idea about what it meant to play as a team despite the fact that they were playing a team game. Unfortunately, this happens a lot more than it should. Direct interaction and communication are ignored in favour of isolated play. Soccer, hockey, basketball, and other team sports are played as though they are individual sports. We saw Phil do this in the very beginning of our work together. I know it seems obvious, but sometimes we forget that individual sports are individual sports, and team sports are team sports. To participate in them in any other way is unhealthy.

We've already seen what can happen when children overindulge in their sport by paying too much attention to isolated play instead of all aspects of the game. When children do not focus on the three forms of Social Interest, the true essence of soccer and other team sports becomes lost. How frustrating must it be to play a "team" sport and know that your teammates are playing it in an "individual" way? Overindulgent children don't realize it, but ignoring direct interaction and communication only robs them of becoming better players and learning invaluable life lessons.

Note to parents: the chances of your children making it to the World Cup of Soccer are, at best, slim. Even if they do make it (and I sincerely hope they do), there is life after an illustrious soccer career. I would like to think that you'd want your children to learn an approach that would serve them well in pro soccer, college, business, or any other facet of life. As I've suggested throughout this entire book, sport is a vehicle for life.

Now, encouragement is perhaps the most effective strategy that you can use with children, both in sports and in life. In our soccer season, we applied encouragement in some very unique ways to help our players benefit beyond the game.

Keeping Parents In The Loop

The first thing that the co-coach and I did to begin the year was hold a parent meeting after our team's first practice. We informed the parents that, in addition to skill-development, we'd be emphasizing team building throughout the entire season. Some of the same concepts discussed in the previous chapters were outlined for parents at this meeting. We talked about instilling a winning-at-the-*right*-costs mindset and the importance of self-improvement and teamwork. The parents showed unanimous support for our season's plan, especially after we assured them that our strategies would benefit their children off the field as well. It was obvious that much of what we said made an impression on them. Some parents even approached us afterwards to comment that they hadn't heard our ideas presented in that way before. We also made sure to invite their questions and their feedback throughout the year.

This meeting was more important than some of us might think. As a coach, when you engage parents in the process, you'll likely see their children progress too. Parents who align themselves with your goals as a coach will ultimately show support for the coaching process. This opens the door for their kids to learn through the coaching process without any parental roadblocks. In addition to parent meetings, we approached other things differently throughout the year, including captaincy, wins and losses, and running laps to name a few.

Top 7 Coaching Tips: INSPIRE

1. *I*nform parents through meetings, newsletters, etc.
2. *N*etwork with other coaches
3. *S*pend time on skill-development
4. *P*repare through coaching clinics and other resources
5. *I*nvite parents to be involved with team planning & functions
6. *R*emember to instill fun
7. *E*ncourage, Encourage, Encourage

Captaincy: A Privilege Or A Right?

It didn't take long for the egos to arise on our team. In the second practice, two of the more talented players got into a disagreement about who was going to be the captain of our squad. Many of these players, including the two who were arguing, had played together on previous teams, so they were pretty comfortable with one another. Quickly realizing this to be a teachable moment, we gathered the group in a circle and asked them to describe the qualities associated with being a captain. With some joking aside, they were pretty honest about what they thought. One player mentioned scoring hat-tricks (3 goals) every game. Although he said it tongue-and-cheek, it definitely opened up the conversation. We agreed that it was unreasonable to expect the captain to score all of the time, so we asked, "What are some other responsibilities?" They had some difficulty coming up with answers. Finally, one player shouted, "Leadership and hard work!" This seemed to get the ball rolling. They began listing qualities such as sportsmanship, helping out, and taking the coin toss. The boys were saying these things to either please us, or they actually knew deep down inside that these traits were important to the game of soccer. Nevertheless, we thanked them for their help in making our decision about captaincy. They seemed a bit confused as to the reason why we were thanking them. We informed them that the list of qualities they had just given us would help us determine who the captains would be from week-to-week. The two players that modelled the list of traits in both games and practices would represent the club as captains in the game to follow. To quash any doubt about the behaviours we were looking for, we mentioned the importance of working hard in practices; getting along with, and helping out teammates; arriving on time for practices and games; and accepting the playing positions they were given without any complaints.

We hoped that our philosophy would reset their entire approach to the game. The objective was for them to find out that payoffs would come, not just from scoring goals, but from effort and teamwork. We were balancing the playing field by using captaincy as a reward that encouraged internal motivation. Each player would have the opportunity to contribute in many different ways and be acknowledged for his contributions from week-to-week. In fact, the three players who served as captains 5 times by the season's end were not the most skilled by any means, but they worked hard every game, did the things that they were asked to do, led the team in drills, and brought a fun approach to every game. The unhealthy me-first attitude was about to lose its grip on our club and be replaced by the more appropriate team-first approach. We didn't want any of our players to be rewarded for believing he was more important than his fellow mates, and by making captaincy a privilege for everybody, rather than a right just for one, this message was about to be received loud and clear.

Chalk Talk: The Reward Board

One of the most successful tools or rewards that I've used for groups of 5 children or more is the reward board. It's a visual board that has a list of all participants' names on it. Basically, the reward board highlights the number of stamps or stars a child has earned for productive behaviour. At the end of the week, the number of stars or stamps beside each name represents the number of times a child's name gets put into a grand prize draw. The child whose name gets drawn wins the grand prize. Everyone actually ends up receiving something, even if it is something simple, such as a lollipop or a pack of gum. The reward board is effective because you "catch children doing good," and you develop internal motivation even though it appears that you don't. Although children may start out participating because they want to earn a stamp or star, in the hopes of winning the valued grand prize, their "good" behaviour is usually maintained without the need for these external rewards, as long as they are being noticed for behaving appropriately. This system of reward is extremely effective for children who are consistently disruptive.

Put Your Best Foot Forward

As many coaches find out, every season is filled with its ups and its downs. The trick is to make sure that your team doesn't get too low after a loss or too high after a win. They need to stay pretty even-keeled. If they "do the best they can," (sound familiar?) that's all you can ask. When you really think about it, there are so many variables in soccer. There's the referee, the field conditions, the weather, and so on, but the only thing players have control over is their own performance. As coaches, this was our attitude throughout the whole season.

After an endless amount of practices, emphasizing skill-development and game strategy, our team was ready for their first game. The boys knew that we would be pleased with them, as long as they put their best foot forward. In our first game, our team played their hearts out despite losing the battle on the score sheet. The final tally was 3-2 for the opposing team. We were true to our word and showed them how proud we were of their efforts. This message had to be delivered at the beginning of the season to set the tone for the rest of the year. Despite all of our practices, nothing cemented a lesson more than actual game experience. When the kids saw how excited we were to see them play so hard, our message of "teamwork" became a little more real to them. Now, of course they wanted to win, but if you've taken anything away from this book, growth and learning have little to do with the win-loss columns in the standings.

The next game was an entirely different story. You'd be hard-pressed to find two coaches so disappointed in their club's effort. Would you have guessed that we won? Well, we did! But in our view, we had lost. In the first game, we had lost to a club that was expected to win the championship, but our team's effort in that game was unmatched by our opponents. In the second game, our win came against a team who played in a lower division, with less skill and experience, and the score was 4-0. Our disappointment in our team's effort came from them resorting to some selfish habits. A few of our players checked their very own teammates away from the ball. Some others tried to dribble through the opposing team without passing. A few of them even argued about who would take free kicks, and pouted when they weren't able to play the positions that they wanted. After the game, we expressed our disappointment in their lack of team play. The parents, at first, were a little confused about our disappointment because the team had won, but then quickly understood what we were trying to instill in their children - the parent meeting at the beginning of the year really came in handy here.

Believe it or not, this experience was not a setback. We actually expected something like this to happen. We were setting the stage for the whole year and were ready for the challenges that the season offered. We wanted to teach our players about the process and about taking care of themselves and each other.

Can Running Laps Lead To Teamwork?

A big part of our practices throughout the season was dedicated to physical conditioning. Whether it was through wind sprints across the field, or running laps around the practice facility, physical conditioning was used to encourage teamwork amongst our group of boys, who were used to playing the game in an individual way.

After the disappointing effort they had put forth in their 4-0 win, we decided to be a little creative with the "laps" they ran in the practice that followed. We timed the very first lap they did. The first player to complete a full lap did it in a minute and a half, and the last person to cross the finish line came in at the two-minute mark. There was a 30-second gap. We mentioned to the group that, "Those who practiced together played together," and it was obvious that they didn't in the last game. The rest of our practice was dedicated to this motto. The team's task was to complete a full lap with no less than 3 seconds between the first runner and the last runner. We informed them that, even if it took the whole practice, they were expected to complete the drill.

On their first try, there was still a 30-second gap. They were asked to run again. On the second lap, there was a 25-second gap. They were asked to run again. There was another 25-second gap. One player, frustrated after finishing first in all lap attempts, said, "Coach, I can't help it if I'm faster than the rest of them." To everyone's surprise, I replied, "This isn't a race. The task is to run *together*, not to race each other. We don't mind if it takes you double the time. You guys are a team and need to start practicing like one." The same player responded by saying, "You mean we could just jog, just as long as we cross the finish line together?" I replied, "Yep, we're glad you figured it out." In the next lap, we instantly saw our players working together. They were encouraging, communicating, and guiding one another. Yes, they were literally *moving together towards a common goal!* They crossed the finish line with a 10 second gap. We congratulated them for their huge improvement and reminded them that the gap needed to be dwindled to 3 seconds. We noticed that the message of working together didn't get through to one player who seemed to be dawdling for most of the last lap. Without singling him out, we mentioned to them that if one player puts his own interests ahead of the team's, everyone will end up suffering. Then some leaders began to emerge. In the next lap, one of the boys directed everyone to grab another player's arm or shoulder in order to stay close. It worked. They found a way to move together and were able to complete the lap with less than a 3-second gap.

While all of this was going on, the parents were made aware of what we were trying to do, and they all showed their full support by clapping and cheering the kids along. The effects of this practice were seen the following weekend. Before our third game, right before kick-off, we reminded our players of the team concept that was hit home in the last practice. The kids did not disappoint. They played to a hard fought 2-2 draw.

It Has Got To Be Fun!

It's pretty easy to overlook the most important part of sports participation: fun. As coaches and parents, we need to remember that our young players are still children who, in order to continue playing the game, need to "enjoy" playing it. Keeping true to this philosophy, we made a point of surprising our team every once in a while. After a series of excellent efforts in practices and games during the middle part of the season, we informed our club, prior to their match against the previous year's champions at that time, that there would be a surprise awaiting them after the game. The parents were pre-warned that we had booked a private area at a local pizza restaurant for a team party, and they were asked to keep it a secret until the game ended. It was important to let our players know about the "surprise" before the game so that, if they had won, they wouldn't have thought that the surprise was *only* because they had won. All we needed to see from our players was the hard work they had shown us over the past few weeks. The game summary, you ask? Well, our club lost 4-1. However, as we expected, they did everything they were asked to do. You could see on their faces how physically spent they actually were. We brought them together for a quick wrap-up immediately after the game, and reminded them about everything they did well. We then sprung it on them that we were going to meet up later at the pizza restaurant. A couple of the boys couldn't believe their ears. One player caught himself asking, "Even though we lost?" But he was quickly reminded of our slogan: "just play hard."

The evening at the restaurant was a blast, and it gave us an excellent chance to do some additional team building. At one point in the party, we engaged in a joke telling session, which ended up being the highlight of the evening. We decided then and there to turn that activity into a team tradition. We made a team decision that for the rest of the season someone would tell a joke to start every practice and every game. It was a neat routine which began at the party and reminded our boys, before they stepped out onto the field, of the fun associated with the game. It was a great way of bringing our players a little closer together.

If you recall, we hinted in the first chapter, that understanding the objective side of sport would help us appreciate the subjective side and fun aspects that much more. If you understood process thinking, I-am messages, and encouragement, you'll understand how the objective and subjective sides of sport go-hand-in-hand. All of these concepts work together to help keep the fun in the game. Our soccer club, at season's end, was living proof. Often, the word "fun" gets thrown around aimlessly when talking about sports, but now we know that it's a vital part of ensuring the healthy overall development of our children.

Putting The "Earning" In Learning

So let's summarize, shall we. As coaches we celebrated some of our losses, showed disappointment in some of our wins, and took the team out for pizza after being blasted on the scoreboard. Why such an unconventional approach? Well, because instilling fun and skill have little to do with the outcome. That's been our message the entire time. Oh, by the way, did I mention that we won the championship that year? Even years after that season ended, parents continued to remind us of the influence that *that* particular soccer year had on their children's growth, both on and off the field.

The season was remembered because of the way we all came together. Our championship was special because everyone was a part of it. There were no superstar mentalities on the team who were heavily relied upon for our team's success. We had a different hero each and every game. When we received our championship trophy, there was a sense that it was "earned" not just "won." We took such pride in our effort, improvement, and teamwork that the trophy was almost secondary. Our boys learned what many professional athletes don't get the chance to learn. They realized the difference between earning a trophy and winning one. When you *earn* a trophy, you *learn* that it's more about the effort it took (the process) than actually getting it (the outcome). In other words, it may be more amazing to earn second place than to win first. Those ads that claim, "You don't win silver, you lose gold" are way off!

What this story boils down to is the definition of success we discussed earlier. It isn't about fame, riches, or even trophies, but more about the way in which we approach the challenges that life has to offer. Thankfully, our players are in a better position to do this now, than they were before, because of a remarkable season that was built around process thinking and encouragement. What a memorable season indeed!

EXTRA INNING:
There Is No Room In Sports For Abuse!

The title of this "Extra Inning" may seem to point out a pretty straightforward message, but the reality is, nothing could be further from the truth. When we witness game officials being attacked, players being hazed or initiated negatively, and sports parents inflicting harm on others, the message obviously isn't being heard. Safety needs to be guaranteed. Sadly enough, safety isn't guaranteed in the sports world and serious changes need to occur to ensure that it is.

The problem is that the parents and coaches who require supervision don't often seek it out. They may even reject the television ad campaigns, seminars, and resources geared specifically towards them. Fortunately, those of us who are proactive can make a difference by shaping the way our children's leagues and associations are run. We can offer effective check systems so that disturbing incidents never happen, or if they do, supports are put in place to eliminate any chance of a re-occurrence.

One of the best ways to extinguish potentially harmful behaviour is through prevention. It seems to be a common tendency for us, as a society, to respond to a situation when it's way too late. Some people argue that preventative measures aren't really cost-effective. My answer: "How do you measure the cost of a parent's life, a referee's health, or a child's well-being?" You can't!

Here are some recommendations. The first one is for leagues to provide visible off-field referees to supervise and monitor crowds. Well-trained volunteers in touch with a supervisor at all times can help keep costs down. This type of measure will minimize problems involving parents, coaches, and referees while games are underway. The second recommendation is to create an ombudsman position. Establishing an independent, third

party to listen to anonymous and confidential griev-
ances (made by coaches, parents, or referees) and offer
workable solutions can be an invaluable resource. The
third recommendation is to develop and refine league
policies and procedures. Well-outlined consequences
for poor behaviour need to be put in writing, distributed, and then signed by every parent and coach in
the league. A simple signature on a piece of paper can
have a profound effect whenever you refer to it, even
after the harmful behaviour occurs. Reminding parents about their signed documents encourages them to
accept the consequences more readily. Consequences,
which I strongly suggest, should include suspensions
from attending games, season-long expulsions, lifetime
bans, and criminal charges if necessary.

I've only offered a few suggestions here because every league deals with different issues and concerns. I
urge all leagues to come up with their own creative
solutions in order to address the safety issues that are
specific to them. Remember, we can never do too
much to guarantee the safety of children and parents.

CHAPTER 6

Going Beyond The Game

If you really think about it, the lessons learned in this book go way beyond the game played on the field. Many of our lessons in sports become our lessons in life. The interesting thing about a life lesson is once you've learned it, you wonder, "How did I ever live without it?" Your new way of thinking becomes a part of your common sense, and you'd be unable to unlearn it even if you tried. The same holds true for the concepts in this book. You may have caught yourself once or twice thinking, "This just makes sense," or "Why haven't I heard this before?"

With learning, it's also fair to expect some growing pains. When you first lace up a pair of ice skates or jump on your first bike, you have to expect to stumble and fall a few times. These so-called "mistakes" or bumps in the road actually lead to greater learning. They present us with growth opportunities, which we can take full advantage of, when we adopt a process thinking approach.

Process thinking, along with focused attention, can help turn any situation into a positive one. The same applies to parenting. It's self-defeating to beat yourself up about the things that you think you are doing "wrong" as a parent. What's more important is your approach and dedication to your child's upbringing. The fact that you've picked up this book indicates that you have your child's best interest at heart, and this is what needs to be the focus. With such a positive outlook, we have a much better chance of dealing with the challenges involved in raising our children. This approach not only helps me get through the numerous challenges that I face in the work I do with kids, but it also inspires greater learning and growth for everyone involved. Below, I'll share some of the positive learning tools that helped me get through some of the difficulties I experienced with Daniel, who if you recall, used the "basketball shoot-out" to move forward, and Sarina, who used soccer to flourish.

Daniel, A Seatbelt Race, And A Slap In The Face

"Smack!" went Daniel's hand on my cheek. The look on his face was one of pure horror when he realized what he had done. "Am I in trouble?" he asked in a quivering voice. Daniel was bordering on tears in shock that he had just hit me. In a calm and caring tone, I replied, "No, you're not in trouble Daniel. I need to tell you, though, that when you feel excited like that, it's important to keep your hands to yourself and use your words instead." With both sadness and relief in his eyes, he nodded his understanding. I continued to say in a positive and calm voice, "You know that we need to end our visit right now, but we can try again tomorrow, okay?" He replied quietly under his breath, "Okay."

Believe it or not, this episode was a huge step forward in our working relationship. Daniel and I had been working together for approximately 3 months. We developed enough of a rapport where Daniel began to not only appear comfortable on our visits together, but according to his foster parents, he actually expressed looking forward to them. Usually, when rapport is beginning to be developed, you'll see a lot more issues arise as the child begins to feel more comfortable and becomes settled into his or her environment. In a way, I expected things such as Daniel's smacking reaction to unfold, and today they did. After leaving the amusement park, where we had spent over 3 hours playing games and going on rides, we headed for the parking lot towards the car. As we had done so very often, once we got into the car, we shouted, "Seatbelt Race!" and then hurried to see who could put on his seatbelt first. In the excitement of it all, Daniel reacted by swatting me right in the face. I could tell that his reaction was a defensive one, done more out of instinct than out of malice, but this unusual occurrence had to be handled in a way that would encourage both growth and learning. In my mind, I understood that there was more than one way to handle this situation, and that it was pretty hard to predict how these things could unfold. But as I said at the start of this chapter, you just have to maintain a process thinking approach and focus your attention on the child in order to inspire growth and learning in tough situations, even this one.

"I Guess You Won't Do That Again!"

When people hear about the seatbelt race incident, they immediately say to me, "I guess you won't do that again!" My response to them, "Actually, I would! In fact, we'll probably have another one soon." You see, I introduced the seatbelt race to Daniel because it served as a symbol of safety and self-care for him. My intention in turning it into a fun, isolated play game was to ensure that any excitement related to safety and self-care for Daniel would be positive. The fact that Daniel reacted in the way he did was not a bad thing. It actually made complete sense. I'll admit it was a bit of a surprise when it actually happened, but, overall, it wasn't a complete shock.

Remember, Daniel had suffered several months of abuse, and any situation related to safety and self-care would have only triggered negative excitement and negative emotions for him. Daniel's reaction to the seatbelt race indicated that he understood, on some level, it represented safety. It also indicated that he was accustomed to unhealthy excitement when in the presence of male authority figures. You could say it was a self-fulfilling prophecy of sorts. Daniel basically created the negative situation he was accustomed to by getting physical with me, a male. As mentioned, there was no malicious intent on Daniel's part. His defensive reaction was sparked by a history of physical abuse in which he was the victim, and at the time of this incident, being in a setting where the threat of violence simply did not exist, Daniel became the aggressor. These points were critical in figuring out how to deal with the incident.

The Car Ride Home

When you're directly involved in your children's activities, you'll find a lot can happen during the car ride or walk home. Many children and parents look forward to some one-on-one time after an event to discuss games, practices, and anything else that comes to mind. Daniel and I were no different. Following our seatbelt race, we had the chance to deal with our incident. For it to be a positive learning experience, two things needed to happen. First, Daniel needed to understand that his "inappropriate" behaviour didn't mean he was a "bad" boy. That's the very reason why I encouraged him to keep his hands to himself and use his words to express his excitement. It was my attempt to focus on his behaviour and link his feelings to more appropriate actions. When children hit others, in the way that Daniel did, it's typical for them to hear things such as, "Don't ever touch me!" and "You're bad!" in an attack of their character. In a child's mind, it's much easier to correct a behaviour than it is to correct his or her character. Children instinctively know that they have a second chance when their behaviour is the focus. Reminding Daniel of our visit scheduled for the next day, guaranteed him a second chance to improve upon his behaviour.

Second, Daniel needed to understand that there were logical consequences to his behaviour instead of physical hurt and pain. If your children don't put away their bicycles after they have used them, they may lose that privilege for a reasonable amount of time. They don't get brutalized for their actions or, in this case, lack of actions. The logical consequence of Daniel's physical reaction was that our session had to end. Daniel was more likely to understand that his reaction was inappropriate by me taking this measure. Healthy learning would not have occurred if we carried on as though nothing had happened, or if I had just "let it slide." He also would not have learned anything positive if I had clouded the situation by being angry, aggressive, or upset. Instead, Daniel would have lost sight of the consequences and viewed my reaction as a punishment, which only would have reinforced his negative view of adult males. With this in mind, our car ride home needed to be a pleasant one. Playing car games and telling funny stories helped to accomplish this. Daniel realized, perhaps for the first time, that no matter how bad things got, they could still end up positive. This message was reinforced in the car with some laughter and joking, despite a return home that was initiated by something inappropriate. Upon Daniel's arrival home, I expressed how much faith I had in his ability to use his words, instead of his hands, the next time we met.

The Day After

The day after an important incident or event is crucial in ensuring that consequences work. It gives us a chance to show that we are consistent in our approach, and that we actually mean what we say. When we don't do this, we indicate to our children that we are not to be taken seriously, and that if they resist enough, they can manipulate the situation to their liking. Our consistency basically helps our children become more accountable for their own behaviours.

Before Daniel and I entered the car on the next visit, I asked him whether he was up for another seatbelt race. He looked at me, smiled, and then said, "Hands to myself, right?" I returned the smile and replied, "You've got it!" This dialogue was necessary because it indicated that I remembered the incident and, in doing so, helped to reinforce the consequences of the seatbelt race. In other words, our conversation acknowledged Daniel's second chance, which encouraged him to be accountable for his behaviour, demonstrated mutual respect, and established a consistent approach from one day to the next.

Handling the situation in this way had an amazing impact on our working relationship. In turning a negative incident into a positive experience, an adult male was becoming a safe figure for this once battered boy. How did I know he was feeling safe? Well, for the very first time since his abuse, Daniel willingly shared stories of the harm inflicted on him. He hadn't done this before with anyone. I was honored.

Top 7 Ways To Foster Healthy Relationships With Your Child

1. Make eye contact; speak at eye level
2. Paraphrase what they say
3. Give them opportunities to make decisions
4. Greet them with smiles everyday
5. Use positive nicknames to create closeness (Sunny instead of Chubby)
6. Be silly with them (make funny faces)
7. Establish limits; give them healthy choices

What You Need To Know About Logical Consequences

For logical consequences to work, they need to be enforced appropriately. It could mean the difference between effective discipline and ineffective discipline. So, to help out when using them with your kids, feel free to check out the comparison between logical consequences and punishment, as well as, the important notation that follows:

Logical Consequences	Punishment
1. Emphasize mutual rights and mutual respect (adult's respectful attitude is key)	1. Emphasizes adult's authority (adult makes demands)
2. Are related to misbehaviour	2. Is not always tied to the logic of the situation
3. Focus on problem, not on child	3. Judges or attacks the child
4. Focus on present and future behaviour	4. Is concerned with past behaviour

5. Are firm, friendly, and caring	5. Is disrespectful, threatens loss of love, is a put-down
6. Offer a child a choice	6. Demands obedience
7. Are reasonably suited to the misbehaviour	7. Is given in anger and may be excessive
8. View an adult as an educator	8. Views an adult as a dictator

Note: Logical consequences offer only one way of dealing with misbehaviour. If you are having trouble thinking of a logical consequence, that in itself may suggest that it is not the appropriate approach. Remember, logical consequences are:

- Related
- Reasonable
- Respectful

(source: *Respectful Responsible Parenting - A Facilitator's Guide* by Terry Lowe, et al., Revised by Beth Johnson)

Sarina's Homework Hassle

Now, although Sarina made huge strides in her soccer career as well as in her personal life, she still struggled with her schoolwork. The problem wasn't getting the homework done (she actually dedicated more time than ever to her studies), it was more about understanding the concepts. This happens quite often. Sometimes children make strides in certain areas but take a while to catch up in other areas. That's when a process thinking approach and dedication to your child's learning goes a long way in helping him or her overcome these sorts of obstacles.

Once Sarina's school ruled out a learning deficit, her mother was confused about what to do. She saw all of the progress that her daughter was making in other aspects of her life and didn't understand why her "youngest" was having so much trouble grasping the concepts she was studying. Believe it or not, Sarina's birth order may have actually accounted for her difficulties, but some more information about her study habits was first needed before any changes could have been made to them. Since Sarina's mother and I had established a great rapport over the past year and a half, she didn't have a problem going over Sarina's homework routine with

me. The most revealing factor was probably the most
mundane one. Sarina's mother revealed that Sarina's eldest sister Sarah helped Sarina with her homework on a
regular basis. Sarah, age 17, was graduating with honors
from high school, and did a lot of tutoring for students
in the lower grades at her school. Small details, for sure,
but very significant ones, as you'll see.

The Magic Of Birth Order

Here's how birth order comes into play. In a family
of 3 or more children, with the age range being no
more than 5 or 6 years, youngest children will usually
experience the following: being indulged or not being taken seriously by parents and older siblings; being
viewed as the baby; using cuteness and charm to their
advantage; and demonstrating a lack of confidence in
their ability. We know that Sarina was able to overcome
these tendencies in soccer, but with her sister being
involved in her studies, she wasn't able to move past
them as quickly as she had hoped. Sarah unwittingly
was indulging Sarina in her schoolwork and, in doing
so, reinforced her lack of confidence in this area. Soccer was the one thing that Sarina did that no one else
in her family did. In other words, there was no parent
or honor roll sibling to indulge her. She had no reason

to assume that she would not be taken seriously in this sport, and once she was given the opportunity to be self-sufficient, she flourished. The same situation had to be created in her academic setting. So I suggested to Sarina's mother that she allow Sarina to attend our homework program to see whether a change in "set-up," away from her well-meaning sister and under the tutelage of our instructors, would make a difference.

After several weeks of not being indulged or babied, Sarina made excellent progress in mathematics, science, and writing. By the time her next report card came, Sarina showed significant improvement in all of her classes except for physical education where she was already maintaining a good average. As you can see, birth order provides us with some guidelines to frame problems and situations (from our children's perspective), and to respond in ways that meet their specific needs. If birth order strategies are utilized throughout our children's upbringing, it can help eliminate problems before they begin.

The Magic Revealed: Birth Order Characteristics And Strategies

As we've seen, birth order characteristics may help us understand our children's typical behaviour patterns, and may help to take a lot of the guesswork out of the issues they face. But the magic doesn't lie in the behaviour patterns dictated by birth order, it actually lies in the strategies used to eliminate these patterns. You see, birth order patterns are born out of negative circumstances. They exist because of the unhealthy competition that occurs between siblings in a family. When positive parenting strategies are used to support healthier co-existence between siblings, the patterns will cease to exist. This is ultimately our goal. It's very important to note, however, that sometimes birth order patterns will not hold true if the family dynamic has been greatly affected by a severe or even a traumatic set of circumstances.

So to assist you in eliminating birth order patterns with your children, I've listed some of the typical characteristics that occur through unhealthy competition, along with some of the positive strategies used to encourage healthier interactions:

Position	Typical Characteristics	Strategies to Consider
First Child	Used to getting a lot of attention	Beware of high expectations; accept child's behaviour; don't expect perfection
	Usually reliable and responsible; tries to live up to parents' standards	Focus on fun of participating, not winning

	Likely to become high achiever; needs to feel right, perfect, superior, in control	Model and teach acceptance of mistakes as opportunities to learn
Second Child (of two)	Motto: Not first, but always trying harder	Refrain from comparisons with oldest; avoid getting involved in sibling fights
	May develop characteristics opposite to older child (may be rebellious and irresponsible if older child is responsible and co-operative)	Focus on positive behaviour and contributions to prevent reinforcing negative view of self
	Is likely more flexible and friendly, less demanding of parents' attention	Encourage different interests and activities from that of older child
Middle Child (of three)	May feel squeezed between competent, older, and cute youngest baby; may be rebellious and uncooperative	Special time alone with child; give focused attention and make eye contact
	Usually exhibits the strongest or weakest personality in the family	Include in planning of family activities and duties
Middle Children (of larger family)	Usually co-operative and reliable	Take time for one-to-one activities and give focused attention
	Not competitive; may be good mediator or diplomat	Help each child to feel special and worthwhile

	Does not expect extra attention or privileges	Find opportunities for each one to contribute
Youngest Child	Often indulged by parents and older siblings; frequently not taken seriously (baby forever)	Encourage self-reliance; refrain from doing for the youngest what he/she can do alone; refrain from referring to as "the baby"
	Enjoys playing; may be self-indulgent and irresponsible	Allow child to resolve own conflicts; allow to learn from consequences
	Knows how to be cute and charming (possibly manipulative)	Give responsibility and expect contributions
	May lack confidence in ability	Avoid emphasis on cuteness
Only Child	Used to being the centre of attention; finds sharing difficult; may be uncooperative if not getting own way	Model and teach sharing; encourage co-operation through co-operative games and problem solving
	May get along better with people older or younger than themselves	Keep your expectations age-appropriate
	May feel incompetent and unsure of self or may be perfectionistic	Provide varied opportunities for interaction with peers i.e. visits with friends, child care, preschool, sleepovers, etc.

(source: Respectful Responsible Parenting - A Facilitator's Guide by Terry Lowe, et al., Revised by Beth Johnson)

Remember, these birth order categories apply to siblings whose age range is approximately 5 or 6 years. If one child is 15 years old and the other child is 7 years old, then their age difference of 8 years makes each an "only child." Also, keep in mind that it's not a child's *actual* birth order that determines his or her birth order behaviour patterns, it's the *perceived* birth order. In other words, a child who was born "second" may view him or herself as a "first" born child due to unique circumstances, and may develop the traits typically associated with being the eldest.

Beware Of The "Default Tendency"

While working with Sarina, I also got to know her family quite well. In fact, I found out that her middle sister Emily experienced something that often goes undetected. She experienced a defensive reaction which I like to call, the "default tendency." If it isn't addressed early, it can be quite damaging.

Emily, age 14, revealed to me that a few years ago, she had a traumatic set of experiences in sports. In her only year of playing basketball, she was frequently ridiculed by her teammates for her lack of ability, which forced her to not try-out for the team the following year. To make things worse, she decided to quit the school volleyball team before the season was half over because she noticed that her volleyball teammates were reacting to her in the same way that her basketball peers did. This was unfortunate for Emily because these types of experiences tend to transform negative I-am messages into I-must messages. Sometimes this transformation results in a child avoiding one type of sport in favour of another type of sport, which further reinforces his or her newly developed I-must messages. This is the default tendency. In Emily's case, her "I am incapable" message quickly changed into an "I must always isolate myself" message. Emily, however, still wanted to be active, and the only sports available to her based on her "I must always isolate myself" message were individual sports. When her family moved locations, Emily joined the school track & field club and concentrated her efforts on long-distance running.

Three points need to be made regarding Emily's default tendency. First, her long-distance running career began with her overindulging in it. To participate in a sport because you need to avoid other sports is unhealthy. Some positive strategies (such as those used with Daniel and Sarina) are required in order to move Emily away from outcome thinking and more towards process thinking. In other words, if Emily's long-distance running career is to become a productive part of her life, and not just a diversion from team or social situations, Social Interest has to be developed. She needs to get to a point where isolated play in long-distance running builds more positive I-am messages, such as "I am self-reliant" and "I am independent," instead of it reinforcing her "I must always isolate myself" message.

Second, there are many children who experience the same type of trauma that Emily encountered, but they resort to avoiding sports altogether. Instead of playing sports, they may decide to overindulge in individual extra-curricular activities, such as solo music lessons and painting. Unfortunately, these children hold the same type of I-must messages as did Emily, and require the same healthy interventions to help them develop a process thinking approach.

Third, as the middle child, we know that Emily's natural tendency may have been to feel squeezed, and she may have demonstrated weak personality traits, such as being timid, giving up easily, and being submissive. With this in mind, I strongly encouraged Emily's mother to increase her one-on-one time with Emily, as well as provide her with opportunities to contribute to the family's planning of activities and outings. Emily's track and field coach was also urged to integrate more direct interaction into her running activities (i.e. relay races), and utilize encouragement to help Emily develop more positive I-am messages. These are only a few of the changes that were made to help Emily minimize her default tendency and develop a healthier mindset.

Chalk Talk: Passion And Consistency

I know that in addition to this book, there are a number of other parenting tools and resources that you may have sifted through. The best advice I can give to you, apart from what we've already discussed, is to rely on your internal strengths and pay close attention to "passion" and "consistency." Applying these concepts will make a big difference in determining the effectiveness of your approach, whichever one you decide to use.

Right from the start, I spoke of passion, and for me, it is a passion for sports, children, and psychology. Interestingly enough, not too many of us refer to passion when the discussion turns to child development. The lack of attention it receives has a lot to do with passion being interpreted as something uncontained and uncontrolled. I agree, there is no room for volatility in the area of childhood development, but this isn't what passion is about. In this book, passion represents something very contained and controlled. It's one of the most honest and revealing positive emotions we could ever experience. Passion is the motivating, or inspiring force behind our dreams becoming realities. It reveals how much we believe in something and tells us that our actions come from a genuine place. Passion has nothing to do with the insecurities that lead to explosive anger and hostility. So, for the academic world to confuse it with these emotions prevents us from using passion in a way that can truly benefit our lives.

So why is passion so important to our approach? Well, children understand its vibrancy at a very young age without having to verbalize it. If we can communicate and connect with our children before even uttering a word, half of our work is done. With a passionate approach, they will be more likely to choose athletic and life pursuits that represent their authentic selves.

The term "consistency" evokes much different emotions than the term "passion," yet they seem to go together. Passion injects enthusiasm and a zest for life into our parenting, coaching, and teaching styles, while consistency adds stability and reliability to them. Despite their contrasting nature, a passionate approach tends to be the more consistent approach. The more we care about something, the more likely we'll follow through with it on a regular basis. Consistency determines whether our strategies are effective or ineffective. The biggest reason for approaches being ineffective is their inconsistent use, and when we send mixed messages to our children through an inconsistent approach, how can they possibly learn the lessons that we teach them? Remember, it typically takes a few weeks to instill any sort of change in a person, so we need to be consistent, at least over this period of time, if we want our kids to receive the appropriate message.

The Final At Bat

Believe it or not, our time together has neared its end, but before you jump out of your seat, let's see what we have in front of us. Personally, I'm excited about our new frame of reference. We may actually begin to name things that we weren't able to name before. "Naming," in a sense, equips us. It allows us to refer to the language of "encouragement" when our kids bring home their report cards. It also lets us point to the "athlete's paradox" and "outcome thinking" when our talented children begin to receive special treatment. Making these concepts a part of our parenting, coaching, and our teaching may even help to take the personal sting out of the feedback that we give to a child or another parent. Instead of our comments being interpreted as personal attacks, we have the advantage of citing the many concepts in this book to validate what we say. Also, for those of us who have a difficult time dealing with me-first individuals, we now have the support and the approach that can help us deal with them more effectively.

At this stage of the chapter, you've probably grown accustomed to reading an "Extra Inning," but it seems more fitting to end by simply thanking you for taking the time to read this book. I sincerely appreciate every moment you've spent on it and look forward to hearing how its principles have impacted your life and the lives of your children. I also find it fitting that Blakey is waving me over to play soccer with him and his friends, so, on behalf of the both of us, may you and your family share amazing moments together and have lots and lots of fun along the way. See ya out on the playing field!

REFERENCES

Accuser to face NBA star for first time in court: [Final Edition]. (2004, March 23). Leader Post, p. C7. Retrieved, from Canadian Newsstand Core database. (Document ID: 593112591).

Avis, W., P. Drysdale, R. Gregg, M. Scargill. *Canadian Senior Dictionary*. Toronto: Gage Educational Publishing, Ltd., 1979.

Beames, T.B. An Introduction to Adlerian Psychology – A Set of Notes to Accompany Course 401. Chicago: Adler School of Professional Psychology, 1996.

Canada Safety Council [online]. "Canada's Silent Tragedy." (n.d.) [Cited April 14, 2005.] <www.safety-council.org>

Centers for Disease Control and Prevention [online].

"Suicide: Fact Sheet."(n.d.) [Cited April 14, 2005.] <www.cdc.gov>

Four charged in steroid scandal: [FINAL C Edition]. (2004, February 13). The Province, p. A63. Retrieved, from Canadian Newsstand Core database. (Document ID: 547527781).

Grunwald, B. & H. McAbee. *Guiding the Family – Practical Counseling Techniques.* 6th ed. Bristol, PA: Accelerated Development, 1995.

Lowe, T., D. Rugg, B. Johnson, J. Cassidy, R. Vandekamp. *Respectful Responsible Parenting – A Facilitator's Guide.* Saskatoon Adlerian Society, 1995. Revised March 3, 2003 by Beth Johnson.

NHL player arrested for murder plot: [Final Edition]. (2004, April 18). The Province, p. A12. Retrieved, from Canadian Newsstand Core database. (Document ID: 623384391).

Raghoobarsingh, S. *The New Game Plan – Moving Towards A Common Goal.* Vancouver: TeamWorks Productions, 2002.

ISBN 142511281-1